D1247906

FREEDOM FROM UNFAIR SEARCHES AND SEIZURES

Other books in this series:

The Bill of Rights

FREEDOM FROM UNFAIR SEARCHES AND SEIZURES

Edited by Robert Winters

Bruce Glassman, *Vice President*
Bonnie Szumski, *Publisher*
Helen Cothran, *Managing Editor*
Scott Barbour, *Series Editor*

GREENHAVEN PRESS
An imprint of Thomson Gale, a part of The Thomson Corporation

THOMSON
™
GALE

Detroit • New York • San Francisco • San Diego • New Haven, Conn.
Waterville, Maine • London • Munich

T 49822

THOMSON

GALE

LIBRARY OF CONGRESS CATALOGING-IN-PUBLICATION DATA

Freedom from unfair searches and seizures / Robert Winters, book editor.
    p. cm. — (Bill of Rights)
Includes bibliographical references and index.
ISBN 0-7377-1927-3 (lib. : alk. paper)
    1. Searches and seizures—United States—History. 2. Searches and seizures—United States. I. Winters, Robert, 1963– . II. Bill of Rights (San Diego, Calif.)

KF9630.Z9F74 2006
345.73'0522—dc22   2005047187

Printed in the United States of America

Chapter Two: The Supreme Court Applies the Fourth Amendment

Chapter Three: Current Perspectives on Search and Seizure

"I cannot agree with those who think of the Bill of Rights as an 18th century straightjacket, unsuited for this age. . . . The evils it guards against are not only old, they are with us now, they exist today."

—Hugo Black, associate justice of the
U.S. Supreme Court, 1937–1971

The Bill of Rights codifies the freedoms most essential to American democracy. Freedom of speech, freedom of religion, the right to bear arms, the right to a trial by a jury of one's peers, the right to be free from cruel and unusual punishment—these are just a few of the liberties that the Founding Fathers thought it necessary to spell out in the first ten amendments to the U.S. Constitution.

While the document itself is quite short (consisting of fewer than five hundred words), and while the liberties it protects often seem straightforward, the Bill of Rights has been a source of debate ever since its creation. Throughout American history, the rights the document protects have been tested and reinterpreted. Again and again, individuals perceiving violations of their rights have sought redress in the courts. The courts in turn have struggled to decipher the original intent of the founders as well as the need to accommodate changing societal norms and values.

The ultimate responsibility for addressing these claims has fallen to the U.S. Supreme Court. As the highest court in the nation, it is the Supreme Court's role to interpret the Constitution. The Court has considered numerous cases in which people have accused government of impinging on their rights. In the process, the Court has established a body of case law and precedents that have, in a sense, defined the Bill of Rights. In doing so, the Court has often reversed itself and introduced new ideas and approaches that have altered the legal meaning of the rights contained in the Bill of Rights. As a general rule, the Court has erred on the side of caution, upholding and expanding the rights of individuals rather than restricting them.

An example of this trend is the definition of cruel and unusual punishment. The Eighth Amendment specifically states, "Excessive bail shall not be required, nor excessive fines imposed, nor cruel and unusual punishments inflicted." However, over the years the Court has had to grapple with defining what constitutes "cruel and unusual punishment." In colonial America, punishments for crimes included branding, the lopping off of ears, and whipping. Indeed, these punishments were considered lawful at the time the Bill of Rights was written. Obviously, none of these punishments are legal today. In order to justify outlawing certain types of punishment that are deemed repugnant by the majority of citizens, the Court has ruled that it must consider the prevailing opinion of the masses when making such decisions. In overturning the punishment of a man stripped of his citizenship, the Court stated in 1958 that it must rely on society's "evolving standards of decency" when determining what constitutes cruel and unusual punishment. Thus the definition of cruel and unusual is not frozen to include only the types of punishment that were illegal at the time of the framing of the Bill of Rights; specific modes of punishment can be rejected as society deems them unjust.

Another way that the Courts have interpreted the Bill of Rights to expand individual liberties is through the process of "incorporation." Prior to the passage of the Fourteenth Amendment, the Bill of Rights was thought to prevent only the federal government from infringing on the rights listed in the document. However, the Fourteenth Amendment, which was passed in the wake of the Civil War, includes the words, ". . . nor shall any state deprive any person of life, liberty, or property, without due process of law; nor deny to any person within its jurisdiction the equal protection of the laws." Citing this passage, the Court has ruled that many of the liberties contained in the Bill of Rights apply to state and local governments as well as the federal government. This process of incorporation laid the legal foundation for the civil rights movement—most specifically the 1954 *Brown v. Board of Education* ruling that put an end to legalized segregation.

As these examples reveal, the Bill of Rights is not static. It truly is a living document that is constantly being reinterpreted and redefined. The Bill of Rights series captures this vital aspect of one of America's most cherished founding texts. Each volume in the series focuses on one particular right protected in the Bill of Rights. Through the use of primary and secondary sources, the right's evolution is traced from colonial times to the present. Primary sources include landmark Supreme Court rulings, speeches by prominent experts, and editorials. Secondary sources include historical analyses, law journal articles, book excerpts, and magazine articles. Each book also includes several features to facilitate research, including a bibliography, an annotated table of contents, an annotated list of relevant Supreme Court cases, an introduction, and an index. These elements help to make the Bill of Rights series a fascinating and useful tool for examining the fundamental liberties of American democracy.

Famed English statesman William Pitt once declared that "the poorest man may, in his cottage, bid defiance to all the forces of the Crown. . . . The wind may blow through it; the storm may enter; the rain may enter; but the King of England may not enter; all his force dare not cross the threshold of the ruined tenement." It was a powerful testament to a highly unusual idea, certainly to eighteenth-century minds: that a man's home was his castle and that he could refuse entry to the king's officials even if they were on legitimate government business.

In the colonies, this idea took hold rather dramatically and helped to spark the American Revolution itself. Frustrated by widespread smuggling in the colonies, the British Parliament created writs of assistance. These orders gave customs officials the right to enter any residence or business at will and search for contraband merchandise; that is, for merchandise on which the colonists had not paid customs duties. The writs also empowered officials to demand the assistance of others to enforce these sweeping powers. The colonists believed that the writs turned them into second-class citizens. The only limitation was that the writs expired on the death of the monarch who issued them, so when George II died in 1760, the colonists had an opportunity to react. When the chief of customs for Boston made a request to the superior court to renew his authority to issue new writs of assistance, the chief justice surprised him by raising doubts about the court's authority to issue them. Instead, the chief justice ordered a hearing to determine the legality of the writs, an unusual imposition by one British official on another.

Even more surprisingly, the attorney general for colonial Massachusetts, James Otis, resigned his office rather than argue on behalf of the writs. In fact, he agreed to appear at the hearing on behalf of a group of Boston merchants who had long opposed the writs and took the opportunity to formally present their case. In an impassioned speech, Otis denounced the writs as tyrannical and hopelessly unenforceable. He averred that the people themselves would not allow the writs to be enforced even if "the King of Great Britain in person were encamped on Boston Common at the head of twenty thousand men." In fact, after consulting with British officials in London, the chief justice found the writs to be legal, but proved Otis right. The people were aroused and outraged, and the writs became increasingly difficult to enforce. Fifty years later, John Adams, the sixth president of the United States, remembered being in the courtroom that day and declared in a letter to a friend, "Every man in a crowded audience appeared to me to go away, as I did, ready to take up arms against Writs of Assistance. Then and there was the first scene of the first act of opposition to the arbitrary claims of Great Britain."

Eventually, of course, those "arbitrary claims" led to the American Revolution and the creation of a new country with a new government. But the old fears remained, and a majority of legislators insisted on a Bill of Rights to limit the potential of the federal government to oppress the people. Many of these legislators remembered the hated writs of assistance and insisted on a Fourth Amendment sharply limiting the national government from conducting searches that would violate the "right of the people to be secure in their persons, houses, papers, and effects." They also insisted on spelling out the provision that warrants must be based on probable cause and must "particularly describ[e] the place to be searched, and the persons or things to be seized."

From Civil Remedy to Procedural Rule

For the founders, the issues of search and seizure were fairly straightforward. In the colonists' view, British customs officials were a despised group enforcing unpopular trade laws designed to keep the colonists from competing with British manufacturers or importing goods from non-British colonies. Customs duties were seen as an example of taxation without representation. It was easy to resent arrogant British officers bursting into the homes and warehouses of prominent merchants who were providing the goods that people desired.

For a self-governing republic, the issues were more complicated. Americans were legitimately afraid that federal officials might act as arbitrarily as their British predecessors but also wanted to ensure that legitimate evidence could be found and used in court. The limited warrants spelled out in the Fourth Amendment were intended to meet both of these goals. To ensure that courts respected these limitations, the citizens of the new nation relied on an old remedy: the civil suit.

In English common law, the source of much American law, individuals could sue an official who violated their right to be protected from unlawful search and seizure. This in fact had happened in a famous eighteenth-century case concerning a radical named John Wilkes, who received monetary damages from a high government official who had violated his rights by seizing some so-called seditious materials with a vague warrant. It was logical to assume that American citizens would have the same recourse to a civil lawsuit if they felt a police official or a judge had violated their Fourth Amendment rights. In fact, this remained an assumption for almost a hundred years because there was no significant Fourth Amendment case for the Supreme Court to rule on. When a case did merit its attention in 1886, the Court proved that assumption incorrect. Instead of accepting the simple civil remedy, the Court laid the groundwork for a new approach that would dramatically change criminal justice procedure: the exclusionary rule.

The Exclusionary Rule

The exclusionary rule has its roots in the 1886 Supreme Court case *Boyd v. United States*. This was a complicated matter that began with a friendly deal. The federal government had allowed a glass-plate importer, Edward Boyd, to import a certain amount of glass duty-free in return for supplying the government with glass he had on hand to help in a construction project that was running behind schedule. The relationship turned ugly when customs officials suspected that Boyd was trying to import more than the agreed-upon amount of duty-free glass, thereby evading import taxes. The customs department not only seized his shipment but also held him liable for fraud. As part of its investigation, the customs department ordered Boyd to produce his invoice. Ultimately he complied, but with a vigorous objection that the order violated his Fifth Amendment right against self-incrimination— that is, his right not to be forced to produce evidence that could be used against him in court.

Since customs duties law was one of the few areas in which the federal government had undisputed jurisdiction, the Supreme Court decided to take Boyd's appeal. It agreed that his Fifth Amendment right against self-incrimination had been violated, but in a controversial ruling, Justice Joseph Bradley went further: He held that compelling Boyd to produce this invoice also constituted an illegal seizure of evidence and was therefore a Fourth Amendment violation as well. By questioning the use of Boyd's own private papers to convict him, Bradley first expressed the idea that certain evidence should be excluded from trial if unlawfully seized. His reasoning was controversial, especially since it seemed to imply that any court subpoena of private papers was illegal. The ruling was also peculiar because the civil forfeiture of Boyd's glass was overturned, but his criminal conviction for fraud was allowed to stand. For the next few decades, the Supreme Court largely ignored these implications of the *Boyd* decision and seemed to imply that evidence could be admitted however obtained.

It was not until *Weeks v. United States*, decided in 1914, that the exclusionary rule that has come to dominate so much of judicial thinking was firmly established. This was the first case in which the Supreme Court actually reversed a conviction because the evidence used during the trial had been obtained during a warrantless search. *Weeks* also went beyond *Boyd* in establishing that even illegal contraband, not just lawful papers, could be excluded as evidence if it was obtained improperly. When the Court decided in *Mapp v. Ohio*, in 1961, that the exclusionary rule must also apply to state courts, this novel rule became a staple of jurisprudence throughout the country.

The Exclusionary Rule in Practice

The exclusionary rule is a powerful testament to the importance of Fourth Amendment privacy rights. At the same time, it has led to frustration for police, prosecutors, and the general public alike when solid cases have evaporated because of a mistake in police procedure or the impracticality of obtaining a warrant. While the Supreme Court still holds that the exclusionary rule is necessary to rein in abuse of police and prosecutors alike, the justices have developed a number of exceptions to accommodate objections. However, these exceptions are themselves subject to clearly defined limitations.

Traditionally, search "incident to arrest" was accepted in common law, and the Court has upheld that practice. Evidence found in pat-downs or other detentions, even for completely unrelated crimes, can be introduced at trial. These searches must be reasonable, however, and strip searches, blood draws, and other invasive procedures need a considerably greater justification than the fact that somebody was detained by a police officer on a vague suspicion. The police also have the right to stop and frisk "suspicious" individuals. Another exception is the plain view doctrine: When police spot evidence in plain sight after being admitted to a home or business, that evidence is admissible. Police officers also have an inherent right to search vehicles that they have pulled over for some legitimate reason based on probable cause. The rationale for this exception is that obtaining a warrant in such cases is impractical: By the time a warrant could be obtained, a suspect in a car could easily flee the scene and dispose of the evidence. In fact, police may use a traffic violation to pull over a car even if their real purpose is to find illegal drugs or stolen property. Again, there are limitations. There are "scope" violations, such as searching a glove compartment under the pretext of finding a missing person. Police may frisk a driver or passenger, but only if they have a reasonable suspicion that the person may be armed.

These are just a few of the ways in which evidence that supposedly violates the exclusionary rule can in fact be admitted based on particular circumstances. Other exceptions are more sweeping. As with other individual rights, there is a general consent exception to the Fourth Amendment; a warrantless search is valid if the suspect consents to it, although prosecutors have the burden of proving that consent was truly voluntary. In addition, appeals courts will not allow defendants to raise Fourth Amendment issues later if they failed to do so during the trial. Moreover, since the 1984 decision in *United States v. Leon*, there is a "good faith" exception in which evidence is allowed if it was obtained under a warrant that police believed was legitimate, even if it was actually defective. They can also be acting in good faith if they execute a warrantless search based on one of the many exceptions, even if that exception is later deemed by a court to be unlawful.

The Question of Privacy

In addition to establishing rules and exceptions for conducting searches, Supreme Court decisions have redefined the traditional understanding of searches, dramatically expanding the scope of the Fourth Amendment. Again, for the founders, the issue seemed simpler. Barging into a home or business and seizing materials and papers is an innately physical act. The *Boyd* decision first raised the possibility that searching might be a more subtle matter by finding that compelling a suspect to provide evidence might constitute a kind of search.

However, it was the decision in *Katz v. United States*, in 1967, that fundamentally changed the nature of searches in American jurisprudence. In an unusual move, the Supreme Court specifically overturned its 1928 precedent in *Olmstead v. United States*, which had found that a warrantless wiretap was legal because it required no physical entry into a private business or residence. This time around, the Court ruled that "the Fourth Amendment protects people, not places." Specifically, the bug on a telephone booth that was used to convict Charles Katz of running an illegal gambling operation violated his rights even though he could not claim that a public telephone booth was his personal property. Instead, in the highly charged words of Justice John Marshall Harlan's concurring opinion, Katz enjoyed "a reasonable expectation of privacy" even in this public place because of the nature of telephone conversations.

The subjective nature of "expectations" combined with the amorphous nature of privacy has opened another wide area of disputes over the Fourth Amendment. People may obviously feel a sense of privacy in their own home, but if they leave out incriminating evidence for any visitor to see, that might mean in effect waiving their privacy concerns. A conversation between friends on a street corner could be private, but suspects having the same conversation in a police car on their way to the station would not enjoy an expectation of privacy by any reasonable standard.

Even more problematic are changes in technology that have fundamentally altered the nature of privacy questions. Just as earlier courts grappled with the dilemma presented by wiretaps, modern jurists must contend with questions raised by more sophisticated electronic surveillance technologies, such as satellite imagery, heat imaging, and Internet search programs. If satellites are recording every inch of U.S. territory, how reasonable is it for citizens to assume a right to privacy even in their own backyards? Is it reasonable to expect any privacy for personal Web logs, for posts to discussion groups, or even for e-mail messages to or from public entities such as corporations? Should FBI agents be conducting sweeping searches of the Internet for words or phrases that may indicate criminal intent, or does that violate the assumption that searches should be based on probable cause? Even more problematic are massive databases kept by government agencies or corporations for legitimate reasons. Should these files be available to criminal investigators, and, if so, under what circumstances? Just how wide a net should officials be allowed to cast in searching for possible criminal behavior?

Fourth Amendment Rights and the War on Terror

In addition to technological developments, changes in the wider culture and in the perceptions of U.S. citizens have also affected Fourth Amendment rights of Americans. In the wake of the September 11, 2001, attacks, many government officials, commentators, and ordinary citizens felt that the nation had gone too far in blocking federal agents and other police forces from rooting out terrorist cells and conspirators. Some provisions, such as forbidding FBI agents from entering mosques to listen in on sermons, were repealed. The Patriot Act repealed a number of other restrictions, such as requiring prior notice before searches. Broad powers to monitor and eavesdrop on foreign citizens without probable cause were extended to American agents in cases involving national security. Some new powers, such as attempts to monitor suspects' conversations with their lawyers or to obtain library records, proved too controversial and were either struck down or voluntarily repudiated. But overall the federal government and some state agencies now have significantly greater search and seizure powers than before 9/11 and a greater determination to use them.

From the beginning, Americans have shown a determination to protect themselves and their property from the intrusions of police and other government officials. The limited and specific warrant, a powerful restriction in itself, has been supplemented by the exclusionary rule in an effort to protect privacy and weigh the validity of evidence. However controversial and difficult they are to define, these provisions are so fully entrenched in the U.S. court system that it is unlikely they would ever be repealed outright.

However, Fourth Amendment rights have always been subjected to numerous limitations that dramatically affect how they work in practice. New technologies and new procedures continually raise practical questions, and the Supreme Court has shown considerable flexibility in weaving between concerns for privacy and for effective police work. In evaluating the new tools in the war on terror, the Court will build on that history. Because of the obvious connection between terrorism and national security, however, the Court may lean toward a restricted view of Fourth Amendment rights. Traditionally, the Court has shown a certain deference to the executive branch when it comes to national security considerations. There is ample precedent for expanding government powers to combat terrorism if the courts choose to find it.

Already, there are programs in place, primarily through the Patriot Act and the creation of the Homeland Security Department, that expand search powers and coordination between intelligence agencies. Under these new provisions, the government can conduct warrantless searches without notification before or after doing so, confiscate property from suspected terrorists, and in certain circumstances spy on citizens without judicial review. There have been calls for even more dramatic expansions, such as the Pentagon's Total Information Awareness database, which would have compiled financial, medical, and travel records on virtually all Americans if Congress had not scuttled it. Other proposals have been advanced, such as allowing government agents to wiretap any phone or monitor anybody's e-mail for fifteen days without warrant or probable cause. It is of course unclear how many of these ideas would survive the political process or court challenges, but it is clear that many search and seizure provisions are being rethought and revised.

For some Americans, the fact that the nation is indisputably under a new and dangerous threat should take priority even over some traditional liberties. They might agree with Justice Arthur Goldberg, who declared in 1963 that "while the Constitution protects against invasions of individual rights, it is not a suicide pact." Others might agree with Benjamin Franklin's comment in 1759: "Those that would give up essential liberty to obtain a little temporary safety deserve neither liberty nor safety." The challenge of balancing individual freedom and collective security is a vital question for the generations coming of age in this century, but they might take comfort from the ability of the Supreme Court to show both sensitivity and a certain amount of imagination in considering both liberty and safety when interpreting the Fourth Amendment.

CHAPTER ONE

Early Developments in Limiting Search and Seizure

The Bill of Rights

English Jurists Limit Search and Seizure

Nelson B. Lasson

The roots of protection from unreasonable searches go back quite far in England. Drawing on Roman and Anglo-Saxon traditions, English kings as far back as Alfred the Great, who reigned in the ninth century, insisted that their judges follow certain procedures in gathering evidence. Still, it is difficult to establish what exactly those procedures were, and it seems that royal officials were often able to ignore them. Over the course of the fourteenth century, English Parliaments began to take a stronger interest in the rights of subjects. In contrast, the Tudor and Stuart monarchs of the fifteenth, sixteenth, and seventeenth centuries often pushed back with oppressive laws and special courts. One such court was the Star Chamber, which could ignore the rights of suspects in pursuit of seditious or treasonous materials. A crisis developed in the seventeenth century when King Charles I attempted to rule without regard to Parliament. Among many grievances, Parliament resented King Charles's use of general searches to seize papers that he found treasonable and to collect taxes that Parliament found unlawful. Ultimately, these disputes led to the English Civil War in the 1640s and the overthrow and execution of King Charles.

In the following selection, Nelson B. Lasson, a lecturer in political science at the University of Maryland, describes the evolution of the right to reasonable search and seizure following the reign of Charles I. Over the course of the seventeenth and eighteenth centuries, members of Parliament and individual printers successfully challenged both kings and courts when their books, private papers, and other ma-

Nelson B. Lasson, *The History and Development of the Fourth Amendment to the United States Constitution.* Baltimore, MD: Johns Hopkins Press, 1937.

terials were seized with the use of general warrants. Such warrants do not specify persons, places, or objects to be searched and seized and therefore grant wide latitude to officers to search and seize at random. By the mid-eighteenth century courts had ruled that such warrants are illegal and that the government must have probable cause to enter a person's home and take his or her property. Thus the principle underlying the Fourth Amendment was established under English common law.

L et us . . . inquire into the state of development of the common law at this period [the seventeenth century] with regard to search and seizure. English jurisprudence it seems had begun to shape itself along more modern lines and conceptions of liberty and justice. The principle that search and seizure must be reasonable, that there must be a balancing of the problems of the administration of justice with those of the freedom of the individual, was emerging slowly and was assuming more and more the character of an underlying concept of jurisprudence. However, before this principle could definitely and finally impress and establish itself in the public mind as a fundamental right of *constitutional* importance, the more spectacular situations present in the eighteenth century were necessary.

Early Attempts to Limit Search and Seizure

In a contemporaneous seventeenth-century treatise on the history of the pleas of the crown by Chief Justice [Matthew] Hale, one of the greatest jurists in English history, the chief limitations upon the exercise of search and seizure now embodied in such constitutional provisions as the Fourth Amendment are already found presented either as law or as recommendations of the better practice, which later hardened into law. For instance, a general warrant to apprehend all persons suspected of having committed a given crime was held by Hale to be void and no defense to a suit for false imprisonment. The party asking for the warrant should be examined under oath touching the whole matter, whether a crime had actually been committed and the reasons for his suspicion. The warrant should specify by name or description the particular person or persons to be arrested and must not be left in general terms or in blanks to be filled in afterwards. Upon the reasoning of the first rule, Hale held that warrants to search any suspected place for stolen goods were invalid (although he admitted that there were precedents of such general warrants) and should be restricted to search in a particular place suspected, after a showing, upon oath, of the suspicion and the "probable cause" thereof, to the satisfaction of the magistrate. "For these warrants," he said, "are judicial acts, and must be granted upon examination of the fact. And therefore, I take these general warrants dormant, which are made many times before any felony committed, are not justifiable, for it makes the party to be in effect the judge; therefore, searches made by pretense of such general warrants give no more power to the officer or party, than what they may do by law without them." It is "convenient," he added, that the precept should express that the search be made in the daytime; that the complainant ought not be given the warrant for execution, although he should be present to give the officer information of his goods; that no doors be broken open; and that the goods should not be delivered to the complainant until so ordered by the court. [English jurist Sir Edward] Coke previously, in a somewhat ambiguous statement, had denied altogether the legality of search warrants for stolen goods. On the question of warrants of arrest "to answer such matters as shall be objected" against the party, Hale wrote that such warrants, notwithstanding earlier precedents of their use, were not regular and anyone so arrested was to be discharged upon habeas corpus.

The Law in Practice

However, these salutary rules of the common law exercised but little influence upon Parliament. In the first year after the Restoration [the reestablishment of the monarchy under Charles II in 1660], it is true, an act to enforce the payment of customs duties did provide for the issuance of special warrants under oath in searches of houses and for full damages and costs against the informer if the information proved to be false. But two years later, several statutes were enacted which were of the same stamp as the legislation of preceding regimes. Incidentally, these statutes were to play leading roles in the events on both sides of the Atlantic that laid the permanent foundation for the principle of reasonable search and seizure. The first was the Licensing Act for the regulation of the press. It made provision for powers of search as broad as any ever granted by Star Chamber[1] decree. The second was an act "to prevent frauds and abuses in the custom." One instrumentality to aid in its enforcement was the general writ of assistance already mentioned. A third statute passed in the same year brought into existence the hated "hearth money," in the collection of which officials were given right of entry into all houses any time during the day.

The Licensing Act expired upon the refusal of Charles II to summon Parliament in 1679. In order not to lose the advantages of this legislation, the king called together the twelve judges of England to decide whether the press could be as effectively regulated by the common law as by the statute. The chief justice was [Sir William] Scroggs, always extremely facile in arriving at any opinion agreeable to the Crown. After resolving that seditious libel was a criminal offense at common law and that such libels could be seized, the judges came to the rather remarkable conclusion that to write, print, or publish any book, pamphlet, or other matter, was illegal without a license from the king. A proclamation was accordingly issued by Charles to suppress seditious libels and unlicensed printing and the chief justice, in turn, upon the basis of the proclamation, issued general warrants of search and arrest to enforce it. In 1680, the activities of Scroggs and his associates were investigated by the House of Commons. Printers and book-sellers hastened to complain of unjust vexation by the messengers of the press armed with these warrants. When Scroggs was impeached, one of the articles of impeachment was based on his issuance of "general

1. The Star Chamber was a court separate from the common law system that meted out punishment while affording few rights to the accused. It was abolished in 1641.

warrants for attaching the persons and seizing the goods of his majesty's subjects, *not named or described particularly*, in the said warrants; by means whereof, many . . . have been vexed, their houses entered into, and they themselves grievously oppressed, contrary to law." Here was a legislative recognition of the idea that general warrants were an arbitrary exercise of governmental authority against which the public had a right to be safeguarded.

Moving Toward Reasonable Search and Seizure

After the Revolution of 1688,[2] another forward step was taken in acknowledgment of this privilege. One of the first acts of the new government, by insistence of King William himself, was to abolish "hearth-money." But what is of most interest here is the reason given for this action. The "hearth-money," declares the preamble of the statute, is not only a great oppression of the poorer classes, "but a badge of slavery upon the whole people, exposing every man's house to be entered into, and searched by persons unknown to him." From this time on through the whole succeeding period there may be noticed a certain tendency in legislation not to grant powers of search and seizure as lavishly as had been the case in former years. . . .

Probably arising out of the practice under the Licensing Act and inadvertently continued when that act failed of reenactment, a usage had grown up for the secretary of state to issue general warrants of search and arrest in seditious libel and similar cases. Strange to say, in all the years between the rejection of the statute in 1695 and the accession of George III in 1760, the validity of these warrants was questioned only once, and then more or less casually. In that instance, in the case of *Rex v. Earbury*, the warrant had directed the seizure of *all* the defendant's papers, but Lord Hardwicke [Chief Justice Philip Yorke, Earl of Hardwicke] had refused to give an opinion on the point on the ground that since he had no authority to order the return of the pa-

2. This uprising replaced Catholic King James II with Protestants William III and Mary II.

pers, the question was not before the court. But it was this continued exercise of power that was destined to lead to the final establishment of the principle of reasonable search and seizure upon a constitutional footing in England and to constitute at the same time one of the main factors in the history of such provisions in American bills of rights.

The Wilkes Case

In 1762, John Wilkes, then a member of Parliament, began to publish anonymously his famous series of pamphlets called the *North Briton*, deriding the ministers and criticizing the policies of the government. This continued until the following year when *Number 45* of this series appeared, containing an unusually bitter attack upon the King's Speech in which, incidentally, among other things, the cider tax had been highly praised. Smarting under the constant and effective censure, the government determined to apprehend and prosecute the responsible party and by the usual procedure. A warrant was issued by Lord Halifax, the secretary of state, to four messengers, ordering them "to make strict and diligent search for the authors, printers, and publishers of a seditious and treasonable paper, entitled, The North Briton, No. 45, . . . and them, or any of them, having found, to apprehend and seize, together with their papers."

Here was a warrant, general as to the persons to be arrested and the places to be searched and the papers to be seized. Of course, probable cause upon oath could necessarily have no place in it since the very questions as to whom the messengers should arrest, where they should search, and what they should seize, were given over into their absolute discretion. Under this "roving commission," they proceeded to arrest upon suspicion no less than forty-nine persons in three days, even taking some from their beds in the middle of the night. Finally, they apprehended the actual printer of *Number 45* and from him they learned that Wilkes was the author of the pamphlet. Wilkes was waiting for just such an opportunity, having on different occasions advised others to resist such warrants. He pronounced the messengers' authority "a ridiculous warrant against the whole English nation" and refused to obey it. The messengers thereupon took him up in a chair and conveyed him in that manner to the office of the secretary of state, after which, accompanied by an undersecretary of state, they returned to the house. Refusing admission to any of Wilkes' friends, they had a blacksmith open the drawers of Wilkes' bureau and took away, uninventoried, all of his private papers including his will and also his pocketbook. Wilkes afterwards was committed to the Tower by the secretary of state upon his refusal to answer questions but was released a few days later upon habeas corpus by reason of his privilege as a member of Parliament.

All the printers, upon the suggestion and with the support of opponents of the government, brought suit against the messengers for false imprisonment. Chief Justice [John] Pratt held the warrant to be illegal. "To enter a man's house by virtue of a nameless warrant," said the Chief Justice, "in order to procure evidence, is worse than the Spanish Inquisition; a law under which no Englishman would wish to live an hour." The London jury awarded the particular plaintiffs in the test cases damages of £300 and the other plaintiffs had verdicts of £200 by consent.

Wilkes Brings Suit

Wilkes brought suit against Wood, the undersecretary who had superintended the execution of the warrant. The Chief Justice this time upheld a verdict of no less than £1000 in favor of the plaintiff. He declared that this warrant was a point of the greatest consequence that he had ever met with in his whole practice.

> The defendants claimed a right under precedents to force persons' houses, break open escritoires, seize their papers, upon a general warrant, where no inventory is made of the things taken away, and where no offenders' names are specified in the warrant, and therefore a discretionary power given to messengers to search wherever their suspicions may chance to fall. If such a power is truly invested in a secretary of state, and he can delegate this power, it certainly may affect

the person and property of every man in this kingdom, and is totally subversive of the liberty of the subject. If higher jurisdictions should declare my opinion erroneous, I submit as will become me, and kiss the rod; but I must say I shall always consider it as a rod of iron for the chastisement of the people of Great Britain.

A suit by Leach, a printer, against the messengers brought him a verdict of £400. Wilkes got a judgment of £4000 against Lord Halifax himself a number of years later. The government undertook the responsibility of defending all actions arising from the warrant and the payment of all judgments. The expenses incurred were said to total £100,000.

These decisions were greeted with the wildest acclaim all over England. "Wilkes and Liberty" became the by-word of the times, even in far-away America. Chief Justice Pratt became one of the most popular men in the country. He was given addresses of thanks in large numbers and presented with the freedom of London, Dublin, and other cities. The city of London requested, in addition, that he sit for his portrait for the famous artist, Sir Joshua Reynolds. When completed, the portrait was hung in Guildhall with an inscription by [famed English lexicographer and author Dr. Samuel Johnson] designating him the "zealous supporter of English liberty by law." Pratt's opinions on the question of general warrants, moreover, were directly responsible for his subsequent elevation to the peerage in 1765 and to the lord chancellorship in 1766. . . .

The Entick Case

In November of 1762, a half year before the *North Briton* incident, Lord Halifax had issued a warrant to the messengers to search for John Entick, author of the *Monitor or British Freeholder*, and seize him together with his books and papers. This warrant was specific as to the person but general as to papers. The messengers in this instance also, as might be expected, made the most of the discretion granted them. Entick at first took no action, but after witnessing the success of Wilkes and the printers, he was encouraged to sue the messengers in trespass for the seizure of his papers. The jury gave him a verdict of £300 damages.

This case was later argued before the Court of Common Pleas. In 1765, Pratt, now Lord Camden, delivered the opinion of the court, an opinion which has since been denominated a landmark of English liberty by the Supreme Court of the United States. "If this point should be decided in favor of the Government," said the court, "the secret cabinets and bureaus of every subject in this kingdom would be thrown open to the search and inspection of a messenger, whenever the secretary of state shall see fit to charge, or even to suspect, a person to be the author, printer, or publisher of a seditious libel." An unreasonable power, the court went on, must have a specific foundation in law in order to be justified. A person's "house is rifled," the court continued, "his most valuable papers are taken out of his possession, before the paper, for which he is charged, is found to be criminal by any competent jurisdiction, and before he is convicted of writing, publishing, or being concerned in the paper. Such is the power, and therefore one should naturally expect that the law to warrant it should be as clear in proportion as the power is exorbitant." The origin of the practice was in Star Chamber days; the Licensing Act had expired; and the usage since the Revolution of issuing these warrants, not based upon any statutory authority, was absolutely illegal. The court, sarcastically referring to the old tribunal consisting of Scroggs and his associates as "a great and reverend authority," denied that they could by their extrajudicial resolution establish in law the general search warrant which, indeed, was so soon thereafter condemned by the House of Commons. To the argument of long usage the court answered: "There has been a submission of guilt and poverty to power and the terror of punishment. But it would be a strange doctrine to assert that all the people of this land are bound to acknowledge that to be universal law, which a few criminal booksellers have been afraid to dispute."

Parliamentary Actions

The subsequent resolutions of the House of Commons with respect to general warrants were largely a result of these two circumstances, the opinions of the judges in the recent cases and the popular feeling on the question. None of the law officers of the Crown defended the legality of the warrant in the course of the parliamentary debate. Charles Yorke, who had been attorney general at the time the warrant was issued, actually protested its legality during the discussion and maintained that he had not been consulted on that question. But to [William] Pitt goes the actual credit of forcing the hand of the Commons in the matter. In February, 1764, when the question was brought up on the floor of the House, he was the central figure in the debate. All that the Crown and the ministers had desired, he declared, had been accomplished in the conviction of Wilkes for libel and his expulsion from Parliament. Now it was the duty of Parliament to do justice to the nation, the constitution, and the law. He denied that precedent afforded any justification. He himself, as secretary of state, had issued similar warrants in 1760, not in mere libel cases, but in cases of emergency arising from the state of war. He knew them to be illegal because his friend Pratt, who was then attorney general, had told him they would be illegal and that he would have to take the consequences. But "preferring the general safety, in time of war and public danger, to every personal consideration, he ran the risk, as he would of his head, had that been the forfeit, upon the like motive."

Pitt's Speech

The government succeeded in postponing the decision on the question only by the barest majority. Two years later, in April, 1766, the House of Commons resolved that general warrants in cases of libel were illegal. But this limited condemnation did not satisfy Pitt. He forced the House to declare that general warrants were universally invalid, except as specifically provided for by act of Parliament, and if executed upon a member of the House, a breach of privilege. But an attempt to introduce a bill to prohibit the seizure of persons by general warrants was turned down. And a bill to restrain the issuance of warrants to seize papers, except in cases of treason and felony without the benefit of clergy, and then under certain regulations, which was passed by the Commons, was rejected by the House of Lords.

One of Pitt's many eloquent remarks on these occasions, a sample of his great oratorical powers, has become classic:

> The poorest man may, in his cottage, bid defiance to all the forces of the Crown. It may be frail; its roof may shake; the wind may blow through it; the storm may enter; the rain may enter; but the King of England may not enter; all his force dares not cross the threshold of the ruined tenement.

In this manner did Pitt express the consummation of the ideal "a man's house is his castle," the subordination of governmental authority to the principle of safeguarded search and seizure.

An American Colonist Opposes General Search Warrants

James Otis

In eighteenth-century England, authorities often violated search-and-seizure protections in an attempt to stamp out publications that they considered treasonable. In the American colonies, the issue was much more likely to be smuggling. It was an open secret that many respectable merchants in New England used smuggling to evade restrictions on trading with Spanish colonies in the West Indies and other areas outside the British Empire. To counter this practice, the British government began to issue "writs of assistance," warrants giving customs officials and their agents the right to search businesses, and later homes, at will. Traditionally, these writs expired on the death of the monarch and were renewed by the next monarch. When George III ascended the throne, the Boston merchants decided to fight the legality of these writs, and they hired James Otis to plead their case. Otis was actually a former advocate general, and thus had once been responsible for enforcing writs of assistance, but he had resigned in 1761 rather than support their renewal. In an impassioned speech before the superior court of Massachusetts, excerpted below, he argued that the writs were illegal, dangerous, and absurd. Otis maintained that because the writs were general warrants that did not specify persons or places to be searched, they gave too much discretion to customs officials and their subordinates to enter people's homes and take their possessions. Despite his eloquent arguments, Otis lost the case.

James Otis, address to the superior court of Boston, MA, February 1761.

In attendance on the day of Otis's speech was a young John Adams, future Founding Father and U.S. president, who took extensive notes. Unfortunately, Otis's speech was not published, but working from Adams's notes, George Richards Minot reproduced much of the speech in his history of Massachusetts, and Adams later corrected this version for a biography of James Otis. Despite the lack of publication, the impact of the speech was clearly enormous on its listeners and on the course of history. Decades later, John Adams declared, "Then and there the child Independence was born."

I was desired by one of the court to look into the books, and consider the question now before them concerning Writs of Assistance. I have accordingly considered it, and now appear, not only in obedience to your order, but likewise in behalf of the inhabitants of this town, who have present another petition, and out of regard to the liberties of the subject. And I take this liberty to declare, that, whether under a fee or not (for in such a cause as this I despise a fee), I will to my dying day oppose, with all the powers and faculties God has given me, all such instruments of slavery on the one hand, and villainy on the other, as this Writ of Assistance is.

It appears to me the worst instrument of arbitrary power, the most destructive of English liberty and the fundamental principles of law, that was ever found in an English law-book. I must, therefore, beg your Honors' patience and attention to the whole range of an argument, that may, perhaps, appear uncommon in many things, as well as to points of learning that are more remote and unusual, that the whole tendency of my design may the more easily be perceived, the conclusions better descend, and the force of them be better felt.

Refusal to Argue Against Liberty

I shall not think much of my pains in this case, as I engaged in it from principle. I was solicited to argue this case as advocate-general; and because I would not, I have been charged with desertion from my office. To this charge I can give a very sufficient answer. I renounced that office, and I argue this case, from the same principle; and I argue it with the greater pleasure, as it is in favor of British liberty, at a time when we hear the greatest monarch upon earth declaring from his throne, that he glories in the name of Briton, and that the privileges of his people are dearer to him than the most valuable prerogatives of his crown; and it is in opposition to a kind of power, the exercise of which, in former periods of English history, cost one king of England his head, and another his throne.[1]

I have taken more pains in this case than I ever will take again, although my engaging in this and another popular case has raised much resentment. But I think I can sincerely declare, that I cheerfully submit myself to every odious name for conscience' sake; and from my soul I despise all those whose guilt, malice or folly, has made them my foes.

Let the consequences be what they will, I am determined to proceed. The only principles of public conduct, that are worthy of a gentleman or a man, are to sacrifice estate, ease, health and applause, and even life, to the sacred calls of his country.

These manly sentiments, in private life, make the good citizen; in public life, the patriot and the hero. I do not say that, when brought to the test, I shall be invincible. I pray God I may never be brought to the melancholy trial; but if ever I should, it will then be known how far I can reduce to practice principles which I know to be founded in truth. In the meantime, I will proceed to the subject of this writ.

General Warrants Are Illegal

Your Honors will find, in the old books concerning the office of a justice of the peace, precedents of general warrants to search suspected houses. But, in more modern books, you will find only special warrants to search such and such houses, specially named, in which the complainant has before sworn, that he suspects his goods are concealed; and will find it adjudged, that special warrants only are legal. In the same manner, I rely in it, that the writ prayed for in this petition,

1. referring to Charles I and James II

being general, is illegal. It is a power that places the liberty of every man in the hands of every petty officer.

I say, I admit that special Writs of Assistance, to search special places, may be granted to certain persons on oath; but I deny that the writ now prayed for can be granted; for I beg leave to make some observations on the writ itself, before I proceed to other acts of Parliament.

In the first place, the writ is universal, being directed to 'all and singular justices, sheriffs, constables, and all other officers and subjects;' so that, in short, it is directed to every subject in the King's dominions. Every one, with this writ, may be a tyrant in a legal manner, and may control, imprison, or murder, any one within the realm.

In the next place it is perpetual; there is no return. A man is accountable to no person for his doings. Every man may reign secure in his petty tyranny, and spread terror and desolation around him, until the trump of the archangel shall excite different emotions in his soul.

In the third place, a person with this writ, in the daytime, may enter all houses, shops, etc., at will, and command all to assist him.

Fourthly, by this writ, not only deputies, etc., but even their menial servants, are allowed to lord it over us. What is this but to have the curse of Canaan with a witness on us? To be the servant of servants, the most despicable of God's creation?

A Man's Home Is His Castle

Now, one of the most essential branches of English liberty is the freedom of one's house. A man's house is his castle; and whilst he is quiet, he is as well guarded as a prince in his castle. This writ, if it should be declared legal, would totally annihilate this privilege. Custom-house officers may enter our houses when they please; we are commanded to permit their entry. Their menial servants may enter, may break locks, bars, and every thing in their way; and whether they break through malice or revenge, no man, no court, can inquire. Bare suspicion, without oath, is sufficient.

This wanton exercise of this power is not a chimerical suggestion of a heated brain. I will mention some facts. Mr. Pew [a customs officer] had one of these writs, and, when Mr. Ware [another customs officer] succeeded him, he endorsed this writ over to Mr. Ware; so that these writs are negotiable from one officer to another; and so your Honors have no opportunity of judging the persons to whom this vast power is delegated. Another instance is this:

Mr. Justice Walley had called this same Mr. Ware before him, by a constable, to answer for a breach of the Sabbath-day acts, or that of profane swearing. As soon as he had finished, Mr. Ware asked him if he had done. He replied, 'Yes.' 'Well, then,' said Mr. Ware, 'I will show you a little of my power. I command you to permit me to search your house for uncustomed goods;' and went on to search the house from the garret to the cellar; and then served the constable in the same manner.

But to show another absurdity in this writ, if it be established, I insist upon it, every person, by the 14th of Charles the Second, has this power, as well as the custom-house officers. The words are, 'It shall be lawful for any person, or persons, authorized,' etc. What a scene does this open. Every man prompted by revenge, ill-humor, or wantonness, to inspect the inside of his neighbor's house, may get a Writ of Assistance. Others will ask it from self-defence; one arbitrary exertion will provoke another, until society be involved in tumult and in blood.

The Original Understanding of the Fourth Amendment

Bradford P. Wilson

The influence of English common law, as summarized in legal scholar William Blackstone's *Commentaries on the Laws of England*, was enormous in the eighteenth and nineteenth centuries. Relying on Blackstone, the founders believed that every right implied a remedy if that right was violated, and generally that remedy already existed in common law. In the following selection, Bradford P. Wilson, a political science professor at Ashland University and executive director of the National Association of Scholars, explains the founders' understanding of the legal remedy that was available to those whose Fourth Amendment rights were violated. Under common law, individuals could sue government officials for "trespass" if they believed they had been subjected to an unreasonable search. The Fourth Amendment affirmed this right and forbade the government from interfering with it. This understanding of the Fourth Amendment held for much of American history, but eventually the Supreme Court allowed for broader remedies, such as the exclusionary rule that banned evidence from being used in trials if it was obtained by means of an unfair search.

To understand what the Founders had in mind for the enforcement of constitutional rights, it is necessary to recall that they understood themselves to be building upon the English legal institutions that had been transplanted to the colonies. With equity existing only in a rudimentary form at the time of the Founding, these legal institutions were primarily those of the common law. It was generally accepted that, where no positively enacted law held otherwise, the common law governed rights and duties.

This circumstance is highly significant for our coming to grips with the peculiar "incompleteness" of those constitutional provisions that pronounce the law regarding certain rights, but are silent as to the legal consequences that result from their violation. As one commentator [law professor Alfred Hill] has argued, "There is no reason to believe that the draftsmen of the Constitution gave specific attention to the problems of implementation. . . . The Constitution was to be implemented in accordance with the remedial institutions of the common law." Although the framers surely did not intend to prohibit legislative action aiding in the enforcement of constitutional rights, such action was not required to complete the Constitution as law in [English jurist William] Blackstone's sense.

Again, relying on our commentator: "It may fairly be assumed that the founding fathers did not contemplate a new species of constitutional tort [i.e., lawsuit]. There is evidence that the transgression of a government officer was regarded as a trespass, in accordance with the vocabulary and outlook of the common law." To regard such transgressions as trespasses is not to limit the corresponding remedy for any manner of abuse to an action in trespass, understood in its strict sense. The term "trespass" in the common law tradition was ordinarily used in a broader sense "to describe the conduct of a government officer actionable at common law, even though strictly speaking a form of action other than trespass would have been appropriate in the particular case" [according to Hill]. The framers' reliance upon the remedial institutions of the common law explains why, although many a legal right could be found on the books without a corresponding remedy being specified, Chief Justice [John] Marshall could confidently assert as binding for the American system of law Blackstone's formulation that "it is a general and indisputable rule, that where there is a legal right, there is also a legal remedy, by suit or action at law, whenever that right is invaded."

The Fourth Amendment Affirmed Common Law

It must be conceded that a difficulty in implementation through actions at law would arise if a right created by the Constitution had no common law counterpart and for which no appropriate common law remedy could be found to exist. The Fourth Amendment, however, is emphatically free of this problem. The language of the amendment does not purport to create the right to be secure against unreasonable searches and seizures, but rather recognizes it as already existing. As was observed by Justice [Joseph] Story, the Fourth Amendment "is little more than the affirmance of a great constitutional doctrine of the common law." An integral part of that "great constitutional doctrine of the common law" was that unreasonable searches and seizures were considered trespasses, and that officers of the government who abused their authority in such a manner were liable to those whose persons or property they caused to be invaded.

That this remedial branch of the common law on the subject of search and seizure was well known to the Fourth Amendment's framers cannot be gainsaid. It was central to the controversy over the legality of general warrants, which arose from the circumstances accompanying the Crown's arrest of John Wilkes for seditious libel during the reign of George III. The search and seizure of the books and papers, and in some instances the persons, of Wilkes and forty-eight other Englishmen under general warrants resulted in "the first and only major litigation in the English courts in the field of search and seizure." The controversy spanned the years 1763 to 1765, and its fame this side of the Atlantic was second only to James Otis's attempt to prevent the issuance to customs officers of writs of assistance, which in their oppressive nature were much akin to the general warrants used in England against Wilkes and his comrades. For our purposes, we need only to note that every action brought by Wilkes and his associates for the unreasonable searches and seizures was for damages against the officials who issued the warrants and the officers who executed them.

When the common law origins of the Fourth Amendment are recognized, and it is further observed that the amendment does not create a right but rather acknowledges an existing one, the amendment does not appear to suffer from incompleteness. For the Fourth Amendment to be law in the full sense, it must be understood as requiring an available remedy for violation of the asserted right. The framers assumed that this demand was met by the remedial aspect of the common law regarding unreasonable searches and seizures.

A Right to Sue Officials

One scholar [Albert J. Harno] has suggested that the Fourth Amendment "guarantees that the injured person shall not be denied a cause of action against the trespasser." This position carries the necessary implication that the abrogation by legislative action of civil remedies for illegal searches and seizures would violate the Fourth Amendment, and presumably due process as well. According to this view, the civil remedy against errant government officers was given constitutional sanction by the Fourth Amendment and cannot lawfully be abridged.

We would agree that, in light of the framers' understanding of the nature of law, the Fourth Amendment must be understood as guaranteeing the availability of a remedy for violations of the Fourth Amendment right; and if Congress should take affirmative action to deny such a remedy, its action would be unconstitutional and void. This is not to say, however, that the Fourth Amendment gives fixed constitutional status to any particular remedy. That the framers assumed that common law remedies would be used to implement the Fourth Amendment right does not in any way imply that those specific remedies were themselves of constitutional status. Not only could other remedies and sanctions be added by governmental action to the forms of action characteristic of the common law trespass remedy. [But also,] in keeping with the general principle that common law must give way to statutory law, Congress could legitimately replace the trespass remedy altogether with a criminal or other action, provided that an effective means of enforcement, in harmony with the purposes of the Fourth Amendment, continued to be available for unreasonable searches and seizures.

The point to be emphasized is that the framers did not regard the Fourth Amendment as impotent in the absence of remedial legislation. The common law remedy of trespass historically had been available for unreasonable searches and seizures, and the Fourth Amendment guaranteed that it would continue to be so unless or until the legislature chose to enact an effective substitute.

The Views of Alexander Hamilton

There is less evidence for the view that the common law understood governmental oppression of individuals to be a public as well as a private wrong, thereby rendering offending officers subject to criminal prosecution by the sovereign power. It is noteworthy, however, that such a view was expressed by [Alexander] Hamilton in *The Federalist*. In the eighty-third number, he attempted to assuage those who were fearful of oppressive modes of collecting the national revenue with the argument that,

> as to the conduct of the officers of the revenue, the provision in favor of trial by jury in criminal cases, will afford the security aimed at. Wilful abuses of a public authority, to the oppression of the subject, and every species of official extortion, are offenses against the government; for which, the persons who commit them, may be indicted and punished according to the circumstances of the case.

When Hamilton wrote this, there was no Fourth Amendment, no national Bill of Rights. The laws establishing the public rights and wrongs referred to must, then, have had their source in the body of common law.

If Hamilton's reading of the common law is correct, the Fourth Amendment should perhaps be read as affirming both private and public rights, with their corresponding modes of redress. Indeed, it could plausibly be argued that the public nature of the right protected by the Fourth Amendment is indicated by the amendment's language. It speaks of "[t]he right of the people." The natural sense of these words implies that the right is not only personal, but also collective or public. Our research, however, has not turned up any American case that has treated the violation of the right protected by the common law and the Fourth Amendment as constituting a public crime in the absence of legislation making it so. Hamilton's assumption that willful abuses of a public authority are of a criminal nature does not, then, appear to have found support in common opinion.

Remedy Beyond Compensation of Injury

Be that as it may, it must be observed that the trespass remedy is not devoid of a public end. So much is manifest in the common law doctrine that recovery can be had beyond compensation for the injury received. This doctrine of punitive or exemplary damages received its definitive justification, later cited in American cases, in the English Case of General Warrants in 1763. In that case, Chief Justice [John] Pratt, later to be Lord Camden, upheld a large damage award for a victim of a trespass by the King's officers. In doing so, he stated:

> [A] jury have it in their power to give damages for more than the injury received. Damages are designed not only as a satisfaction to the injured person, but likewise as a punishment to the guilty, to deter from any such proceeding for the future and as a proof of the detestation of the jury to the action itself.

Thus, the remedy the Founding generation considered appropriate for a violation of the Fourth Amendment right, that of trespass, served as redress, punishment, deterrence, and morality.

CHAPTER TWO

The Supreme Court Applies the Fourth Amendment

The Court Establishes the Exclusionary Rule

William R. Day

Traditionally, drawing on English common law, courts had allowed prosecutors to use evidence that had been obtained illegally. Defendants could sue for the return of any property that was seized without a proper warrant, but district attorneys often used their discretion to hold on to evidence they needed at trial. The Supreme Court's 1914 decision in *Weeks v. United States* set a new precedent regarding the use of illegally obtained evidence. When Fremont Weeks was arrested on suspicion of running an illegal lottery through the mail, officers immediately went to his boardinghouse to search his room, despite the lack of a search warrant. Later they returned with a federal marshal, again without a warrant, and seized papers, books, clothes, and other articles. Claiming that his Fourth Amendment rights had been violated, Weeks sued and demanded the return of his property. As Justice William R. Day recounts in the following excerpt, from the Supreme Court's majority opinion, the district attorney returned part of Weeks's property but held on to a number of incriminating documents. Over Weeks's strong objections, the court allowed these documents into evidence, and ultimately Weeks was convicted. He appealed his conviction all the way to the Supreme Court.

The Supreme Court found that documents, even incriminating documents, should not be allowed into evidence if they were seized illegally. In doing so, it effectively created what has come to be called the exclusionary rule, which excludes improperly seized evidence from use in trials. At first this restriction applied only to federal officials and federal

William R. Day, majority opinion, *Weeks v. United States,* U.S. Supreme Court, February 24, 1914.

courts. But as with most other provisions of the Bill of Rights, the rule has been applied to state courts and police, especially since the *Mapp v. Ohio* decision in 1961.

Day served on the U.S. Supreme Court from 1903 to 1922.

The defendant was arrested by a police officer, so far as the record shows, without warrant, at the Union Station in Kansas City, Missouri, where he was employed by an express company. Other police officers had gone to the house of the defendant, and being told by a neighbor where the key was kept, found it and entered the house. They searched the defendant's room and took possession of various papers and articles found there, which were afterwards turned over to the United States marshal. Later in the same day police officers returned with the marshal, who thought he might find additional evidence, and, being admitted by someone in the house, probably a boarder, in response to a rap [knock], the marshal searched the defendant's room and carried away certain letters and envelopes found in the drawer of a chiffonier. Neither the marshal nor the police officer had a search warrant. The defendant filed in the cause before the time for trial [a] petition [for the return of his property]. . . .

Upon consideration of the petition the court entered in the cause an order directing the return of such property as was not pertinent to the charge against the defendant, but denied the petition as to pertinent matter, reserving the right to pass upon the pertinency at a later time. In obedience to the order the district attorney returned part of the property taken, and retained the remainder, concluding a list of the latter with the statement that, 'all of which last above described property is to be used in evidence in the trial of the above-entitled cause, and pertains to the alleged sale of lottery tickets of the company above named.'

After the jury had been sworn and before any evidence had been given, the defendant again urged his petition for the return of his property, which was denied by the court. Upon the introduction of such papers during the trial, the defendant objected on the ground that the papers had been obtained without a search warrant, and by breaking open his home, in violation of the 4th and 5th Amendments to the Constitution of the United States, which objection was overruled by the court. Among the papers retained and put in evidence were a number of lottery tickets and statements with reference to the lottery, taken at the first visit of the police to the defendant's room, and a number of letters written to the defendant in respect to the lottery, taken by the marshal upon his search of the defendant's room.

The defendant assigns error, among other things, in the court's refusal to grant his petition for the return of his property, and in permitting the papers to be used at the trial.

The Question Before the Court

It is thus apparent that the question presented involves the determination of the duty of the court with reference to the motion made by the defendant for the return of certain letters, as well as other papers, taken from his room by the United States marshal, who, without authority of process, if any such could have been legally issued, visited the room of the defendant for the declared purpose of obtaining additional testimony to support the charge against the accused, and, having gained admission to the house, took from the drawer of a chiffonier found there certain letters written to the defendant, tending to show his guilt. These letters were placed in the control of the district attorney, and were subsequently produced by him and offered in evidence against the accused at the trial. The defendant contends that such appropriation of his private correspondence was in violation of rights secured to him by the 4th and 5th Amendments to the Constitution of the United States. We shall deal with the 4th Amendment, which provides:

'The right of the people to be secure in their persons, houses, papers, and effects, against unreasonable searches and seizures, shall not be violated, and no warrants shall issue but upon probable cause, supported by oath or affirmation, and particularly describing the place to be searched, and the persons or things to be seized.'

History of the 4th Amendment

The history of this Amendment is given with particularity in the opinion of Mr. Justice [Joseph] Bradley, speaking for the court in *Boyd v. United States* [1886]. As was there shown, it took origin in the determination of the framers of the Amendments to the Federal Constitution to provide for that instrument a Bill of Rights, securing to the American people, among other things, those safeguards which had grown up in England to protect the people from unreasonable searches and seizures, such as were permitted under the general warrants issued under authority of the government, by which there had been invasions of the home and privacy of the citizens, and the seizure of their private papers in support of charges, real or imaginary, made against them. Such practices had also received sanction under warrants and seizures under the so-called writs of assistance, issued in the American colonies. Resistance to these practices had established the principle which was enacted into the fundamental law in the 4th Amendment, that a man's house was his castle, and not to be invaded by any general authority to search, and seize his goods and papers. . . .

The effect of the 4th Amendment is to put the courts of the United States and Federal officials, in the exercise of their power and authority, under limitations and restraints as to the exercise of such power and authority, and to forever secure the people, their persons, houses, papers, and effects, against all unreasonable searches and seizures under the guise of law. This protection reaches all alike, whether accused of crime or not, and the duty of giving to it force and effect is obligatory upon all intrusted under our Federal system with the enforcement of the laws. The tendency of those who execute the criminal laws of the country to obtain conviction by means of unlawful seizures and enforced confessions, the latter often obtained after subjecting accused persons to unwarranted practices destructive of rights secured by the Federal Constitution, should find no sanction in the judgments of the courts, which are charged at all times with the support of the Constitution, and to which people of all conditions have a right to appeal for the maintenance of such fundamental rights.

What, then, is the present case? . . . The case in the aspect in which we are dealing with it involves the right of the court in a criminal prosecution to retain for the purposes of evidence the letters and correspondence of the accused, seized in his house in his absence and without his authority, by a United States marshal holding no warrant for his arrest and none for the search of his premises. The accused, without awaiting his trial, made timely application to the court for an order for the return of these letters, as well of other property. This application was denied, the letters retained and put in evidence, after a further application at the beginning of the trial, both applications asserting the rights of the accused under the 4th and 5th Amendments to the Constitution. If letters and private documents can thus be seized and held and used in evidence against a citizen accused of an offense, the protection of the 4th Amendment, declaring his right to be secure against such searches and seizures, is of no value, and, so far as those thus placed are concerned, might as well be stricken from the Constitution. The efforts of the courts and their officials to bring the guilty to punishment, praiseworthy as they are, are not to be aided by the sacrifice of those great principles established by years of endeavor and suffering which have resulted in their embodiment in the fundamental law of the land. The United States marshal could only have invaded the house of the accused when armed with a warrant issued as required by the Constitution, upon sworn information, and describing with reasonable particularity the thing for which the search was to be made. Instead, he acted without sanction of law, doubtless prompted by the desire to bring further proof to the aid of the government, and under color of his office undertook to make a seizure of private papers in direct violation of the constitutional prohibition against such action. Under such circumstances, without sworn information and particular description, not even an order of court would have justified such procedure; much less was it within the authority of the United States marshal to thus invade the house and privacy of the accused. In *Adams v. New York* [1914], this court said that the 4th Amendment was intended to secure the citizen in person and property against unlawful invasion of the sanctity of his home by officers of the law, acting under legislative or judicial sanction. This protection is equally extended to the action of the government and officers of the law acting under it. To sanction such proceedings would be to affirm by judicial decision a manifest neglect, if not an open defiance, of the prohibitions of the Constitution, intended for the protection of the people against such unauthorized action.

Adams v. New York

The court before which the application was made in this case recognized the illegal character of the seizure, and ordered the return of property not in its judgment competent to be offered at the trial, but refused the application of the accused to turn over the letters, which were afterwards put in evidence on behalf of the government. While there is no opinion in the case, the court in this proceeding doubtless relied upon what is now contended by the government to be the correct rule of law under such circumstances, that the letters having come into the control of the court, it would not inquire into the manner in which they were obtained, but, if competent, would keep them and permit their use in evidence. Such proposition, the government asserts, is conclusively established by certain decisions of this court, the first of which is *Adams v. New York*. In that case the plaintiff in error had been convicted in the supreme court of the state of New York for having in his possession certain gambling paraphernalia used in the game known as policy, in violation of the Penal Code of New York. At the trial certain papers, which had been seized by police officers executing a search warrant for the discovery and seizure of policy slips, and which had been found in addition to the policy slips, were offered in evidence over his objection. The conviction was affirmed by the court of appeals of New York [in *People v. Adams*], and the case was brought here for alleged violation of the 4th and 5th Amendments to the Constitution of the United States. Pretermitting [i.e., disregarding] the question whether these Amendments applied to the action of the states, this court proceeded to examine the alleged violations of the 4th and 5th Amendments, and put its decision

upon the ground that the papers found in the execution of the
search warrant, which warrant had a legal purpose in the attempt to find gambling paraphernalia, was competent evidence against the accused, and their offer in testimony did not
violate his constitutional privilege against unlawful search or
seizure, for it was held that such incriminatory documents
thus discovered were not the subject of an unreasonable search
and seizure, and in effect that the same were incidentally
seized in the lawful execution of a warrant, and not in the
wrongful invasion of the home of a citizen, and the unwarranted seizure of his papers and property. It was further held
. . . that it was no valid objection to the use of the papers that
they had been thus seized, and that the courts in the course of
a trial would not make an issue to determine that question,
and many state cases were cited supporting that doctrine.

The same point had been ruled in *People v. Adams*, from
which decision the case was brought to this court, where it
was held that if the papers seized in addition to the policy
slips were competent evidence in the case, as the court held
they were, they were admissible in evidence at the trial, the
court saying: 'The underlying principle obviously is that the
court, when engaged in trying a criminal cause, will not take
notice of the manner in which witnesses have possessed
themselves of papers, or other articles of personal property,
which are material and properly offered in evidence.' This
doctrine thus laid down by the New York court of appeals and
approved by this court, that a court will not, in trying a criminal cause, permit a collateral issue to be raised as to the
source of competent testimony, has the sanction of so many
state cases that it would be impracticable to cite or refer to
them in detail. . . . After citing numerous cases the editor
says: 'The underlying principle of all these decisions obviously is, that the court, when engaged in the trial of a criminal action, will not take notice of the manner in which a
witness has possessed himself of papers or other chattels,
subjects of evidence, which are material and properly offered
in evidence. Such an investigation is not involved necessarily
in the litigation in chief, and to pursue it would be to halt in
the orderly progress of a cause, and consider incidentally a

question which has happened to cross the path of such litigation, and which is wholly independent thereof.'

It is therefore evident that the *Adams* Case affords no authority for the action of the court in this case, when applied to in due season for the return of papers seized in violation of the Constitutional Amendment. The decision in that case rests upon incidental seizure made in the execution of a legal warrant, and in the application of the doctrine that a collateral issue will not be raised to ascertain the source from which testimony, competent in a criminal case, comes.

Precedents for 4th Amendment Protection

The government also relies upon *Hale v. Henkel*, in which the previous cases of *Boyd v. United States*, and *Adams v. New York*, *Interstate Commerce Commission v. Brimson*, and *Interstate Commerce Commission v. Baird* are reviewed, and wherein it was held that a subpoena duces tecum [a command to a witness to produce documents] requiring a corporation to produce all its contracts and correspondence with no less than other companies, as well as all letters received by the corporation from thirteen other companies, located in different parts of the United States, was an unreasonable search and seizure within the 4th Amendment, and it was there stated that 'an order for the production of books and papers may constitute an unreasonable search and seizure within the 4th Amendment. While a search ordinarily implies a quest by an officer of the law, and a seizure contemplates a forcible dispossession of the owner, still, as was held in the *Boyd* Case, the substance of the offense is the compulsory production of private papers, whether under a search warrant or a subpoena duces tecum, against which the person, be he individual or corporation, is entitled to protection.' If such a seizure under the authority of a warrant supposed to be legal, constitutes a violation of the constitutional protection, a fortiori does the attempt of an officer of the United States, the United States marshal, acting under color of his office, without even the sanction of a warrant, constitute an invasion of the rights within the protection afforded by the 4th Amendment. . . .

The right of the court to deal with papers and documents in the possession of the district attorney and other officers of the court, and subject to its authority, was recognized in *Wise v. Henkel*. That papers wrongfully seized should be turned over to the accused has been frequently recognized in the early as well as later decisions of the courts.

We therefore reach the conclusion that the letters in question were taken from the house of the accused by an official of the United States, acting under color of his office, in direct violation of the constitutional rights of the defendant; that having made a seasonable application for their return, which was heard and passed upon by the court, there was involved in the order refusing the application a denial of the constitutional rights of the accused, and that the court should have restored these letters to the accused. In holding them and permitting their use upon the trial, we think prejudicial error was committed. As to the papers and property seized by the policemen, it does not appear that they acted under any claim of Federal authority such as would make the amendment applicable to such unauthorized seizures. The record shows that what they did by way of arrest and search and seizure was done before the finding of the indictment in the Federal court; under what supposed right or authority does not appear. What remedies the defendant may have against them we need not inquire, as the 4th Amendment is not directed to individual misconduct of such officials. Its limitations reach the Federal government and its agencies. . . . It results that the judgment of the court below must be reversed, and the case remanded for further proceedings in accordance with this opinion.

The Exclusionary Rule Is Applied to the States

Thomas Campbell Clark

The 1914 Supreme Court decision in *Weeks v. United States* firmly established the exclusionary rule, which forbade the use of illegally obtained evidence in court. However, the practical effect of this ruling was limited because the *Weeks* decision applied only to federal officials and federal courts. Most crimes were investigated by state and local police and tried in state courts, where prosecutors were not bound by the exclusionary rule. The 1961 case *Mapp v. Ohio* extended the application of the exclusionary rule to state courts. While the Bill of Rights had originally applied only to Congress and federal officers, from 1925 onward the Supreme Court began to find that certain rights and provisions were fundamental to the due process of law and therefore applied to state governments as well as the federal government.

In his majority opinion in *Mapp v. Ohio*, Justice Thomas Campbell Clark declared that the provisions of the Fourth Amendment, including the exclusionary rule, were among those fundamental due process concerns. He concluded that the failure to apply the exclusionary rule to states permitted an inconsistent application of justice and invited violations of individual liberties.

Clark was U.S. attorney general under Harry S. Truman and served as a U.S. Supreme Court justice from 1949 to 1967.

A ppellant stands convicted of knowingly having had in her possession and under her control certain lewd and lascivious books, pictures, and photographs in violation of 2905.34 of Ohio's Revised Code. As officially stated in the

Thomas Campbell Clark, majority opinion, *Mapp v. Ohio*, U.S. Supreme Court, June 19, 1961.

syllabus to its opinion, the Supreme Court of Ohio found that her conviction was valid though "based primarily upon the introduction in evidence of lewd and lascivious books and pictures unlawfully seized during an unlawful search of defendant's home. . . ."

The Search and the Trial

Oh May 23, 1957, three Cleveland police officers arrived at appellant's residence in that city pursuant to information that "a person [was] hiding out in the home, who was wanted for questioning in connection with a recent bombing, and that there was a large amount of policy paraphernalia being hidden in the home." Miss Mapp and her daughter by a former marriage lived on the top floor of the two-family dwelling. Upon their arrival at that house, the officers knocked on the door and demanded entrance but appellant, after telephoning her attorney, refused to admit them without a search warrant. They advised their headquarters of the situation and undertook a surveillance of the house.

The officers again sought entrance some three hours later when four or more additional officers arrived on the scene. When Miss Mapp did not come to the door immediately, at least one of the several doors to the house was forcibly opened and the policemen gained admittance. Meanwhile Miss Mapp's attorney arrived, but the officers, having secured their own entry, and continuing in their defiance of the law, would permit him neither to see Miss Mapp nor to enter the house. It appears that Miss Mapp was halfway down the stairs from the upper floor to the front door when the officers, in this highhanded manner, broke into the hall. She demanded to see the search warrant. A paper, claimed to be a warrant, was held up by one of the officers. She grabbed the "warrant" and placed it in her bosom. A struggle ensued in which the officers recovered the piece of paper and as a result of which they handcuffed appellant because she had been "belligerent" in resisting their official rescue of the "warrant" from her person. Running roughshod over appellant, a policeman "grabbed" her, "twisted [her] hand," and she "yelled [and] pleaded with him" because "it was hurting."

Appellant, in handcuffs, was then forcibly taken upstairs to her bedroom where the officers searched a dresser, a chest of drawers, a closet and some suitcases. They also looked into a photo album and through personal papers belonging to the appellant. The search spread to the rest of the second floor including the child's bedroom, the living room, the kitchen and a dinette. The basement of the building and a trunk found therein were also searched. The obscene materials for possession of which she was ultimately convicted were discovered in the course of that widespread search.

At the trial no search warrant was produced by the prosecution, nor was the failure to produce one explained or accounted for. At best, "There is, in the record, considerable doubt as to whether there ever was any warrant for the search of defendant's home." The Ohio Supreme Court believed a "reasonable argument" could be made that the conviction should be reversed "because the 'methods' employed to obtain the [evidence] . . . were such as to 'offend "a sense of justice,'" "but the court found determinative the fact that the evidence had not been taken "from defendant's person by the use of brutal or offensive physical force against defendant."

The State [Ohio] says that even if the search were made without authority, or otherwise unreasonably, it is not prevented from using the unconstitutionally seized evidence at trial, citing *Wolf v. Colorado* (1949), in which this Court did indeed hold "that in a prosecution in a State court for a State crime the Fourteenth Amendment does not forbid the admission of evidence obtained by an unreasonable search and seizure." On this appeal, of which we have noted probable jurisdiction, it is urged once again that we review that holding.

The *Boyd* Precedent

Seventy-five years ago, in *Boyd v. United States* (1886), considering the Fourth and Fifth Amendments as running "almost into each other" on the facts before it, this Court held that the doctrines of those Amendments

apply to all invasions on the part of the government and its employees of the sanctity of a man's home and the privacies of life. It is not the breaking of his doors, and the rummaging of his drawers, that constitutes the essence of the offence; but it is the invasion of his indefeasible right of personal security, personal liberty and private property. . . . Breaking into a house and opening boxes and drawers are circumstances of aggravation; but any forcible and compulsory extortion of a man's own testimony or of his private papers to be used as evidence to convict him of crime or to forfeit his goods, is within the condemnation . . . [of those Amendments].

The Court noted that

constitutional provisions for the security of person and property should be liberally construed. . . . It is the duty of courts to be watchful for the constitutional rights of the citizen, and against any stealthy encroachments thereon.

In this jealous regard for maintaining the integrity of individual rights, the Court gave life to [James] Madison's prediction that "independent tribunals of justice . . . will be naturally led to resist every encroachment upon rights expressly stipulated for in the Constitution by the declaration of rights." Concluding, the Court specifically referred to the use of the evidence there seized as "unconstitutional."

Weeks Establishes the Exclusionary Rule

Less than 30 years after *Boyd*, this Court, in *Weeks v. United States* (1914), stated that

the Fourth Amendment . . . put the courts of the United States and Federal officials, in the exercise of their power and authority, under limitations and restraints [and] . . . forever secure[d] the people, their persons, houses, papers and effects against all unreasonable searches and seizures under the guise of law . . . and the duty of giving to it force and effect is obligatory upon all entrusted under our Federal system with the enforcement of the laws.

Specifically dealing with the use of the evidence unconstitutionally seized, the Court concluded:

> If letters and private documents can thus be seized and held and used in evidence against a citizen accused of an offense, the protection of the Fourth Amendment declaring his right to be secure against such searches and seizures is of no value, and, so far as those thus placed are concerned, might as well be stricken from the Constitution. The efforts of the courts and their officials to bring the guilty to punishment, praiseworthy as they are, are not to be aided by the sacrifice of those great principles established by years of endeavor and suffering which have resulted in their embodiment in the fundamental law of the land.

Finally, the Court in that case clearly stated that use of the seized evidence involved "a denial of the constitutional rights of the accused." Thus, in the year 1914, in the *Weeks* case, this Court "for the first time" held that "in a federal prosecution the Fourth Amendment barred the use of evidence secured through an illegal search and seizure." This Court has ever since required of federal law officers a strict adherence to that command which this Court has held to be a clear, specific, and constitutionally required—even if judicially implied—deterrent safeguard without insistence upon which the Fourth Amendment would have been reduced to "a form of words" [Holmes, *Silverthorne Lumber Co. v. United States* (1920)]. It meant, quite simply, that "conviction by means of unlawful seizures and enforced confessions . . . should find no sanction in the judgments of the courts . . ." [*Weeks v. United States*], that such evidence "shall not be used at all" [*Silverthorne Lumber Co. v. United States*].

Wolf v. Colorado

In 1949, 35 years after *Weeks* was announced, this Court, in *Wolf v. Colorado*, again for the first time, discussed the effect of the Fourth Amendment upon the States through the operation of the Due Process Clause of the Fourteenth Amendment. It said: "We have no hesitation in saying that were a

State affirmatively to sanction such police incursion into privacy it would run counter to the guaranty of the Fourteenth Amendment."

Nevertheless, after declaring that the "security of one's privacy against arbitrary intrusion by the police" is "implicit in the concept of ordered liberty and as such enforceable against the States through the Due Process Clause," and announcing that it "stoutly adhered" to the *Weeks* decision, the Court decided that the *Weeks* exclusionary rule would not then be imposed upon the States as "an essential ingredient of the right." The Court's reasons for not considering essential to the right to privacy, as a curb imposed upon the States by the Due Process Clause, that which decades before had been posited as part and parcel of the Fourth Amendment's limitation upon federal encroachment of individual privacy, were bottomed on factual considerations.

While they are not basically relevant to a decision that the exclusionary rule is an essential ingredient of the Fourth Amendment as the right it embodies is vouchsafed against the States by the Due Process Clause, we will consider the current validity of the factual grounds upon which *Wolf* was based.

Flaws in the *Wolf* Decision

The Court in *Wolf* first stated that "the contrariety of views of the States" on the adoption of the exclusionary rule of *Weeks* was "particularly impressive" and, in this connection, that it could not "brush aside the experience of States which deem the incidence of such conduct by the police too slight to call for a deterrent remedy . . . by overriding the [States'] relevant rules of evidence." While in 1949, prior to the *Wolf* case, almost two-thirds of the States were opposed to the use of the exclusionary rule, now, despite the *Wolf* case, more than half of those since passing upon it, by their own legislative or judicial decision, have wholly or partly adopted or adhered to the *Weeks* rule. Significantly, among those now following the rule is California, which, according to its highest court, was "compelled to reach that conclusion because other remedies have completely failed to secure compliance with the constitutional provisions . . ." [*People v. Cahan* (1955)]. In connection with this California case, we note that the second basis elaborated in *Wolf* in support of its failure to enforce the exclusionary doctrine against the States was that "other means of protection" have been afforded "the right to privacy." The experience of California that such other remedies have been worthless and futile is buttressed by the experience of other States. The obvious futility of relegating the Fourth Amendment to the protection of other remedies has, moreover, been recognized by this Court since *Wolf*.

Likewise, time has set its face against what *Wolf* called the "weighty testimony" of *People v. Defore* (1926). There Justice (then Judge) [Benjamin N.] Cardozo, rejecting adoption of the *Weeks* exclusionary rule in New York, had said that "[t]he Federal rule as it stands is either too strict or too lax." However, the force of that reasoning has been largely vitiated by later decisions of this Court. These include the recent discarding of the "silver platter" doctrine which allowed federal judicial use of evidence seized in violation of the Constitution by state agents, *Elkin v. United States* (1960); the relaxation of the formerly strict requirements as to standing to challenge the use of evidence thus seized, so that now the procedure of exclusion, "ultimately referable to constitutional safeguards," is available to anyone even "legitimately on [the] premises" unlawfully searched, *Jones v. United States* (1960); and, finally, the formulation of a method to prevent state use of evidence unconstitutionally seized by federal agents, *Rea v. United States* (1956). Because there can be no fixed formula, we are admittedly met with "recurring questions of the reasonableness of searches," but less is not to be expected when dealing with a Constitution, and, at any rate, "reasonableness is in the first instance for the [trial court] . . . to determine," *United States v. Rabinowitz* (1950).

It, therefore, plainly appears that the factual considerations supporting the failure of the *Wolf* Court to include the *Weeks* exclusionary rule when it recognized the enforceability of the right to privacy against the States in 1949, while not basically relevant to the constitutional consideration, could not, in any analysis, now be deemed controlling. . . .

The Exclusionary Rule Applies to the States

Since the Fourth Amendment's right of privacy has been declared enforceable against the States through the Due Process Clause of the Fourteenth, it is enforceable against them by the same sanction of exclusion as is used against the Federal Government. Were it otherwise, then just as without the *Weeks* rule the assurance against unreasonable federal searches and seizures would be "a form of words," valueless and undeserving of mention in a perpetual charter of inestimable human liberties, so too, without that rule the freedom from state invasions of privacy would be so ephemeral and so neatly severed from its conceptual nexus with the freedom from all brutish means of coercing evidence as not to merit this Court's high regard as a freedom "implicit in the concept of ordered liberty" [Cardozo, *Palko v. Connecticut* (1937)]. At the time that the Court held in *Wolf* that the Amendment was applicable to the States through the Due Process Clause, the cases of this Court, as we have seen, had steadfastly held that as to federal officers the Fourth Amendment included the exclusion of the evidence seized in violation of its provisions. Even *Wolf* "stoutly adhered" to that proposition. The right to privacy, when conceded operatively enforceable against the States, was not susceptible of destruction by avulsion of the sanction upon which its protection and enjoyment had always been deemed dependent under the *Boyd, Weeks* and *Silverthorne* cases. Therefore, in extending the substantive protections of due process to all constitutionally unreasonable searches—state or federal—it was logically and constitutionally necessary that the exclusion doctrine—an essential part of the right to privacy—be also insisted upon as an essential ingredient of the right newly recognized by the *Wolf* case. In short, the admission of the new constitutional right by *Wolf* could not consistently tolerate denial of its most important constitutional privilege, namely, the exclusion of the evidence which an accused had been forced to give by reason of the unlawful seizure. To hold otherwise is to grant the right but in reality to withhold its privilege and enjoyment. Only last year [1960] the Court itself recognized that the purpose of the exclusionary rule "is to deter—to compel respect for the constitutional guaranty in the only effectively available way—by removing the incentive to disregard it" [*Elkins v. United States*].

Indeed, we are aware of no restraint, similar to that rejected today, conditioning the enforcement of any other basic constitutional right. The right to privacy, no less important than any other right carefully and particularly reserved to the people, would stand in marked contrast to all other rights declared as "basic to a free society" [*Wolf v. Colorado*]. This Court has not hesitated to enforce as strictly against the States as it does against the Federal Government the rights of free speech and of a free press, the rights to notice and to a fair, public trial, including, as it does, the right not to be convicted by use of a coerced confession, however logically relevant it be, and without regard to its reliability. And nothing could be more certain than that when a coerced confession is involved, "the relevant rules of evidence" are overridden without regard to "the incidence of such conduct by the police," slight or frequent. Why should not the same rule apply to what is tantamount to coerced testimony by way of unconstitutional seizure of goods, papers, effects, documents, etc.? We find that, as to the Federal Government, the Fourth and Fifth Amendments and, as to the States, the freedom from unconscionable invasions of privacy and the freedom from convictions based upon coerced confessions do enjoy an "intimate relation" in their perpetuation of "principles of humanity and civil liberty [secured] . . . only after years of struggle" [*Bram v. United States* (1897)]. They express "supplementing phases of the same constitutional purpose—to maintain inviolate large areas of personal privacy" [*Feldman v. United States* (1944)]. The philosophy of each Amendment and of each freedom is complementary to, although not dependent upon, that of the other in its sphere of influence—the very least that together they assure in either sphere is that no man is to be convicted on unconstitutional evidence.

Removing the Double Standard

Moreover, our holding that the exclusionary rule is an essential part of both the Fourth and Fourteenth Amendments is not only the logical dictate of prior cases, but it also makes very good sense. There is no war between the Constitution and common sense. Presently, a federal prosecutor may make no use of evidence illegally seized, but a State's attorney across the street may, although he supposedly is operating under the enforceable prohibitions of the same Amendment. Thus the State, by admitting evidence unlawfully seized, serves to encourage disobedience to the Federal Constitution which it is bound to uphold. Moreover, as was said in *Elkins*, "the very essence of a healthy federalism depends upon the avoidance of needless conflict between state and federal courts." Such a conflict, hereafter needless, arose this very Term, in *Wilson v. Schnettler* (1961), in which, and in spite of the promise made by *Rea*, we gave full recognition to our practice in this regard by refusing to restrain a federal officer from testifying in a state court as to evidence unconstitutionally seized by him in the performance of his duties. Yet the double standard recognized until today hardly put such a thesis into practice. In non-exclusionary States, federal officers, being human, were by it invited to and did, as our cases indicate, step across the street to the State's attorney with their unconstitutionally seized evidence. Prosecution on the basis of that evidence was then had in a state court in utter disregard of the enforceable Fourth Amendment. If the fruits of an unconstitutional search had been inadmissible in both state and federal courts, this inducement to evasion would have been sooner eliminated. There would be no need to reconcile such cases as *Rea* and *Schnettler*, each pointing up the hazardous uncertainties of our heretofore ambivalent approach. . . .

The ignoble shortcut to conviction left open to the State tends to destroy the entire system of constitutional restraints on which the liberties of the people rest. Having once recognized that the right to privacy embodied in the Fourth Amendment is enforceable against the States, and that the right to be secure against rude invasions of privacy by state officers is, therefore, constitutional in origin, we can no longer permit that right to remain an empty promise. Because it is enforceable in the same manner and to like effect as other basic rights secured by the Due Process Clause, we can no longer permit it to be revocable at the whim of any police officer who, in the name of law enforcement itself, chooses to suspend its enjoyment. Our decision, founded on reason and truth, gives to the individual no more than that which the Constitution guarantees him, to the police officer no less than that to which honest law enforcement is entitled, and, to the courts, that judicial integrity so necessary in the true administration of justice.

The judgment of the Supreme Court of Ohio is reversed and the cause remanded for further proceedings not inconsistent with this opinion.

Warrantless Wiretapping Is Ruled Constitutional

William Howard Taft

During the Prohibition era of the 1920s, FBI agents put wiretaps on telephones frequently used by Roy Olmstead, a Washington state bootlegger suspected of smuggling liquor from Canada. As it turned out, the FBI was correct. Olmstead presided over a massive smuggling operation, and agents were able to listen in on numerous conversations with his customers, suppliers, and partners. Transcripts of these conversations were the primary evidence against Olmstead and his partners, who were convicted of conspiracy to violate Prohibition law. Olmstead appealed, claiming that the wiretaps violated his Fourth Amendment protections against warrantless searches and his Fifth Amendment right against self-incrimination.

In *Olmstead v. United States* (1928) the Supreme Court ruled that the Fourth Amendment did not forbid wiretapping. Previous decisions had barred government officials from going through letters sent by or to defendants without a warrant, but in his ruling chief justice William Howard Taft held that telephone conversations were different. For one thing, the government had control over mail delivery, so it had a unique opportunity to abuse this power to search personal correspondence at will. More importantly, seizing papers and letters often required a physical trespass into somebody's home, or at least their mailbox. Neither of these factors applied to telephones or wiretaps, in the opinion of the Court.

The Court's opinion established, at least for a time, that some sort of physical entry or physical seizure was necessary to claim a Fourth Amendment violation. Or, as some put it,

William Howard Taft, majority opinion, *Olmstead v. United States,* U.S. Supreme Court, June 4, 1928.

the Fourth Amendment applies to persons, places, and things, but does not establish an abstract right to privacy. The *Olmstead* decision has been effectively overturned by more recent decisions, especially *Katz v. United States* (1967). However, it remains interesting as an alternative interpretation of the Fourth Amendment, one that guided the courts for decades and that still has its proponents in the legal community.

Chief Justice Taft is the only former U.S. president to have served on the Supreme Court. He served from 1921 to 1930.

The information which led to the discovery of the conspiracy and its nature and extent was largely obtained by intercepting messages on the telephones of the conspirators by four federal prohibition officers. Small wires were inserted along the ordinary telephone wires from the residences of four of the petitioners and those leading from the chief office. The insertions were made without trespass upon any property of the defendants. They were made in the basement of the large office building. The taps from house lines were made in the streets near the houses.

The gathering of evidence continued for many months. Conversations of the conspirators, of which refreshing stenographic notes were currently made, were testified to by the government witnesses. They revealed the large business transactions of the partners and their subordinates. Men at the wires heard the orders given for liquor by customers and the acceptances; they became auditors of the conversations between the partners. All this disclosed the conspiracy charged in the indictment. Many of the intercepted conversations were not merely reports, but parts of the criminal acts. The evidence also disclosed the difficulties to which the conspirators were subjected, the reported news of the capture of vessels, the arrest of their men, and the seizure of cases of liquor in garages and other places. It showed the dealing by Olmstead, the chief conspirator, with members of the Seattle police, the messages to them which secured the release of arrested members of the conspiracy, and also direct promises to officers of payments as soon as opportunity offered.

The Fourth Amendment provides:

The right of the people to be secure in their persons, houses, papers, and effects, against unreasonable searches and seizures, shall not be violated, and no warrants shall issue, but upon probable cause, supported by oath or affirmation, and particularly describing the place to be searched, and the persons or things to be seized.

And the Fifth: 'No person . . . shall be compelled in any criminal case to be a witness against himself.' It will be helpful to consider the chief cases in this court which bear upon the construction of these amendments.

The Precedent of *Boyd*

Boyd v. United States [1886] was an information filed by the District Attorney in the federal court in a cause of seizure and forfeiture against 35 cases of plate glass, which charged that the owner and importer, with intent to defraud the revenue, made an entry of the imported merchandise by means of a fraudulent or false invoice. It became important to show the quantity and value of glass contained in 29 cases previously imported. The fifth section of the Act of June 22, 1874, provided that, in cases not criminal under the revenue laws, the United States attorney, whenever he thought an invoice, belonging to the defendant, would tend to prove any allegation made by the United States, might by a written motion, describing the invoice and setting forth the allegation which he expected to prove, secure a notice from the court to the defendant to produce the invoice, and, if the defendant refused to produce it, the allegations stated in the motion should be taken as confessed, but if produced the United States attorney should be permitted, under the direction of the court, to make an examination of the invoice, and might offer the same in evidence. This act had succeeded the act of 1887, which provided in such cases the District Judge, on affidavit of any person interested, might issue a warrant to the marshal to enter the premises where the invoice was and take possession of it and hold it subject to the order of the judge.

This had been preceded by the act of 1863 of a similar tenor, except that it directed the warrant to the collector instead of the marshal. The United States attorney followed the act of 1874 and compelled the production of the invoice.

The court held the act of 1874 repugnant to the Fourth and Fifth Amendments. As to the Fourth Amendment, Justice [Joseph P.] Bradley said:

> But, in regard to the Fourth Amendment, it is contended that, whatever might have been alleged against the constitutionality of the acts of 1863 and 1867, that of 1874, under which the order in the present case was made, is free from constitutional objection, because it does not authorize the search and seizure of books and papers, but only requires the defendant or claimant to produce them. That is so; but it declares that if he does not produce them, the allegations which it is affirmed they will prove shall be taken as confessed. This is tantamount to compelling their production; for the prosecuting attorney will always be sure to state the evidence expected to be derived from them as strongly as the case will admit of. It is true that certain aggravating incidents of actual search and seizure, such as forcible entry into a man's house and searching amongst his papers, are wanting, and to this extent the proceeding under the act of 1874 is a mitigation of that which was authorized by the former acts; but it accomplishes the substantial object of those acts in forcing from a party evidence against himself. It is our opinion, therefore, that a compulsory production of a man's private papers to establish a criminal charge against him, or to forfeit his property, is within the scope of the Fourth Amendment to the Constitution, in all cases in which a search and seizure would be; because it is a material ingredient, and effects the sole object and purpose of search and seizure.

Concurring, Mr. Justice [Samuel] Miller and Chief Justice [Morrison R.] Waite said that they did not think the machinery used to get this evidence amounted to a search and seizure, but they agreed that the Fifth Amendment had been violated.

The statute provided an official demand for the production of a paper of document by the defendant, for official search and use as evidence on penalty that by refusal he should be conclusively held to admit the incriminating character of the document as charged. It was certainly no straining of the language to construe the search and seizure under the Fourth Amendment to include such official procedure.

The *Weeks* Case

The next case, and perhaps the most important is *Weeks v. United States* [1914], a conviction for using the mails to transmit coupons or tickets in a lottery enterpise. The defendant was arrested by a police officer without a warrant. After his arrest, other police officers and the United States marshal went to his house, got the key from a neighbor, entered the defendant's room, and searched it, and took possession of various papers and articles. Neither the marshal nor the police officers had a search warrant. The defendant filed a petition in court asking the return of all his property. The court ordered the return of everything not pertinent to the charge, but denied return of relevant evidence. After the jury was sworn, the defendant again made objection, and on introduction of the papers contended that the search without warrant was a violation of the Fourth and Fifth Amendments, and they were therefore inadmissible. This court held that such taking of papers by an official of the United States, acting under color of his office, was in violation of the constitutional rights of the defendant and upon making seasonable application he was entitled to have them restored, and that by permitting their use upon the trial the trial court erred.

The opinion cited with approval language of Mr. Justice [Stephen J.] Field in *Ex parte Jackson* [1877], saying that the Fourth Amendment as a principle of protection was applicable to sealed letters and packages in the mail, and that, consistently with it, such matter could only be opened and examined upon warrants issued on oath or affirmation particularly describing the thing to be seized. . . .

There is no room in the present case for applying the Fifth Amendment, unless the Fourth Amendment was first violated. There was no evidence of compulsion to induce the defendants to talk over their many telephones. They were continually and voluntarily transacting business without knowledge of the interception. Our consideration must be confined to the Fourth Amendment.

Application of the *Weeks* Decision

The striking outcome of the *Weeks* Case and those which followed it was the sweeping declaration that the Fourth Amendment, although not referring to or limiting the use of evidence in court, really forbade its introduction, if obtained by government officers through a violation of the amendment. Theretofore many had supposed that under the ordinary common-law rules, if the tendered evidence was pertinent, the method of obtaining it was unimportant. This was held by the Supreme Judicial Court of Massachusetts in *Commonwealth v. Dana*. There it was ruled that the only remedy open to a defendant whose rights under a state constitutional equivalent of the Fourth Amendment had been invaded was by suit and judgment for damages, as Lord Camden held in [the 1765 British case of] *Entick v. Carrington*. Mr. Justice Bradley made effective use of this case in *Boyd v. United States*. But in the *Weeks* Case, and those which followed, this court decided with great emphasis and established as the law for the federal courts that the protection of the Fourth Amendment would be much impaired, unless it was held that not only was the official violator of the rights under the amendment subject to action at the suit of the injured defendant, but also that the evidence thereby obtained could not be received.

The well-known historical purpose of the Fourth Amendment, directed against general warrants and writs of assistance, was to prevent the use of governmental force to search a man's house, his person, his papers, and his effects, and to prevent their seizure against his will. This phase of the misuse of governmental power of compulsion is the emphasis of the opinion of the court in the *Boyd* Case. This appears, too, in the *Weeks* Case. . . .

The amendment itself shows that the search is to be of material things—the person, the house, his papers, or his effects. The description of the warrant necessary to make the proceeding lawful is that it must specify the place to be searched and the person or things to be seized.

The Fourth Amendment Does Not Apply to Telephone Messages

It is urged that the language of Mr. Justice Field in *Ex parte Jackson*, already quoted, offers an analogy to the interpretation of the Fourth Amendment in respect of wire tapping. But the analogy fails. The Fourth Amendment may have proper application to a sealed letter in the mail, because of the constitutional provision for the Postoffice Department and the relations between the government and those who pay to secure protection of their sealed letters. . . . Revised Statutes, 3978 to 3988, whereby Congress monopolizes the carriage of letters and excludes from that business everyone else, and section 3929 (39 USCA 259), which forbids any postmaster or other person to open any letter not addressed to himself. It is plainly within the words of the amendment to say that the unlawful rifling by a government agent of a sealed letter is a search and seizure of the sender's papers of effects. The letter is a paper, an effect, and in the custody of a government that forbids carriage, except under its protection.

The United States takes no such care of telegraph or telephone messages as of mailed sealed letters. The amendment does not forbid what was done here. There was no searching. There was no seizure. The evidence was secured by the use of the sense of hearing and that only. There was no entry of the houses or offices of the defendants. By the invention of the telephone 50 years ago, and its application for the purpose of extending communications, one can talk with another at a far distant place.

The language of the amendment cannot be extended and expanded to include telephone wires, reaching to the whole world from the defendant's house or office. The intervening wires are not part of his house or office, any more than are the highways along which they are stretched. . . .

Only Congress Can Change This

Congress may, of course, protect the secrecy of telephone messages by making them, when intercepted, inadmissible in evidence in federal criminal trials, by direct legislation, and thus depart from the common law of evidence. But the courts may not adopt such a policy by attributing an enlarged and unusual meaning to the Fourth Amendment. The reasonable view is that one who installs in his house a telephone instrument with connecting wires intends to project his voice to those quite outside, and that the wires beyond his house, and messages while passing over them, are not within the protection of the Fourth Amendment. Here those who intercepted the projected voices were not in the house of either party to the conversation.

Neither the cases we have cited nor any of the many federal decisions brought to our attention hold the Fourth Amendment to have been violated as against a defendant, unless there has been an official search and seizure of his person or such a seizure of his papers or his tangible material effects or an actual physical invasion of his house 'or curtilage' for the purpose of making a seizure.

We think, therefore, that the wire tapping here disclosed did not amount to a search or seizure within the meaning of the Fourth Amendment.

Objections Answered

What has been said disposes of the only question that comes within the terms of our order granting certiorari in these cases. But some of our number, departing from that order, have concluded that there is merit in the twofold objection, overruled in both courts below, that evidence obtained through intercepting of telephone messages by government agents was inadmissible, because the mode of obtaining it was unethical and a misdemeanor under the law of Washington. To avoid any misapprehension of our views of that objection we shall deal with it in both of its phases.

While a territory, the English common law prevailed in Washington, and thus continued after her admission in 1889. The rules of evidence in criminal cases in courts of the United

States sitting there consequently are those of the common law. . . .

The common-law rule is that the admissibility of evidence is not affected by the illegality of the means by which it was obtained. Professor [Simon] Greenleaf, in his work on Evidence [*A Treatise on the Law of Evidence*], says:

> It may be mentioned in this place, that though papers and other subjects of evidence may have been illegally taken from the possession of the party against whom they are offered, or otherwise unlawfully obtained, this is no valid objection to their admissibility, if they are pertinent to the issue. The court will not take notice how they were obtained, whether lawfully or unlawfully, nor will it form an issue, to determine that question. . . .

The rule is supported by many English and American cases. . . . The *Weeks* Case announced an exception to the common-law rule by excluding all evidence in the procuring of which government officials took part by methods forbidden by the Fourth and Fifth Amendments. Many state courts do not follow the *Weeks* Case. . . . The common-law rule must apply in the case at bar.

Evidence Obtained Unethically Is Often Admitted

Nor can we, without the sanction of congressional enactment, subscribe to the suggestion that the courts have a discretion to exclude evidence, the admission of which is not unconstitutional, because unethically secured. This would be at variance with the common-law doctrine generally supported by authority. There is no case that sustains, nor any recognized textbook that gives color to, such a view. Our general experience shows that much evidence has always been receivable, although not obtained by conformity to the highest ethics. The history of criminal trials shows numerous cases of prosecutions of oathbound conspiracies for murder, robbery, and other crimes, where officers of the law have disguised themselves and joined the organizations, taken the oaths, and given themselves every appearance of active members engaged in the promotion of crime for the purpose of securing evidence. Evidence secured by such means has always been received.

A standard which would forbid the reception of evidence, if obtained by other than nice ethical conduct by government officials, would make society suffer and give criminals greater immunity than has been known heretofore. In the absence of controlling legislation by Congress, those who realize the difficulties in bringing offenders to justice may well deem it wise that the exclusion of evidence should be confined to cases where rights under the Constitution would be violated by admitting it.

The Fourth Amendment Protects People's Private Communications

Potter Stewart

The 1967 *Katz v. United States* decision is an unusually clear example of the Supreme Court reversing itself. In 1928, in *Olmstead v. United States*, the Court had ruled that wiretaps did not require search warrants because there was no physical trespass or physical seizure of evidence involved. In full compliance with this precedent, FBI agents used a listening device on a public phone booth to monitor the conversations of Charles Katz, who was suspected of running an illegal gambling operation. These conversations were used to convict Katz, and his appeal based on the Fourth Amendment was duly rejected by the court of appeals. The Supreme Court took up the case and ruled that the *Olmstead* decision was no longer valid. In the Court's majority opinion, excerpted here, Potter Stewart explains that the Fourth Amendment protects people from unfair searches and seizures anywhere. They are entitled to expect privacy. A person using a pay phone has the right to assume he is having a private conversation, according to Stewart. Therefore, the government has no right to eavesdrop on that conversation without a search warrant based on probable cause.

Stewart served on the Supreme Court from 1959 to 1981.

The petitioner [Charles Katz] was convicted in the District Court for the Southern District of California under an eight-count indictment charging him with transmitting wagering information by telephone from Los Angeles to Miami

Potter Stewart, majority opinion, *Katz v. United States,* U.S. Supreme Court, December 18, 1967.

and Boston, in violation of a federal statute. At trial the Government was permitted, over the petitioner's objection, to introduce evidence of the petitioner's end of telephone conversations, overheard by FBI agents who had attached an electronic listening and recording device to the outside of the public telephone booth from which he had placed his calls. In affirming his conviction, the Court of Appeals rejected the contention that the recordings had been obtained in violation of the Fourth Amendment, because "there was no physical entrance into the area occupied by [the petitioner]." We granted certiorari [an order by a superior court to a lower court for records of a case] in order to consider the constitutional questions thus presented.

The petitioner has phrased those questions as follows:

A. Whether a public telephone booth is a constitutionally protected area so that evidence obtained by attaching an electronic listening recording device to the top of such a booth is obtained in violation of the right to privacy of the user of the booth.

B. Whether physical penetration of a constitutionally protected area is necessary before a search and seizure can be said to be violative of the Fourth Amendment to the United States Constitution.

The Fourth Amendment Protects People, Not Places

We decline to adopt this formulation of the issues. In the first place, the correct solution of Fourth Amendment problems is not necessarily promoted by incantation of the phrase "constitutionally protected area." Secondly, the Fourth Amendment cannot be translated into a general constitutional "right to privacy." That Amendment protects individual privacy against certain kinds of governmental intrusion, but its protections go further, and often have nothing to do with privacy at all. Other provisions of the Constitution protect personal privacy from other forms of governmental invasion. But the protection of a person's general right to privacy—his right to be let alone by other people—is, like the protection of his property and of his very life, left largely to the law of the individual States.

Because of the misleading way the issues have been formulated, the parties have attached great significance to the characterization of the telephone booth from which the petitioner placed his calls. The petitioner has strenuously argued that the booth was a "constitutionally protected area." The Government has maintained with equal vigor that it was not. But this effort to decide whether or not a given "area," viewed in the abstract, is "constitutionally protected" deflects attention from the problem presented by this case. For the Fourth Amendment protects people, not places. What a person knowingly exposes to the public, even in his own home or office, is not a subject of Fourth Amendment protection. But what he seeks to preserve as private, even in an area accessible to the public, may be constitutionally protected. . . .

The Government stresses the fact that the telephone booth from which the petitioner made his calls was constructed partly of glass, so that he was as visible after he entered it as he would have been if he had remained outside. But what he sought to exclude when he entered the booth was not the intruding eye—it was the uninvited ear. He did not shed his right to do so simply because he made his calls from a place where he might be seen. No less than an individual in a business office, in a friend's apartment, or in a taxicab, a person in a telephone booth may rely upon the protection of the Fourth Amendment. One who occupies it, shuts the door behind him, and pays the toll that permits him to place a call is surely entitled to assume that the words he utters into the mouthpiece will not be broadcast to the world. To read the Constitution more narrowly is to ignore the vital role that the public telephone has come to play in private communication.

Olmstead and *Goldman* Are No Longer Valid

The Government contends, however, that the activities of its agents in this case should not be tested by Fourth Amendment requirements, for the surveillance technique they employed involved no physical penetration of the telephone booth from which the petitioner placed his calls. It is true that the

absence of such penetration was at one time thought to fore-
close further Fourth Amendment inquiry [*Olmstead v. United
States, Goldman v. United States*], for that Amendment was
thought to limit only searches and seizures of tangible property. But "[t]he premise that property interests control the
right of the Government to search and seize has been discredited" [*Warden v. Hayden*]. Thus, although a closely divided
Court supposed in *Olmstead* that surveillance without any
trespass and without the seizure of any material object fell
outside the ambit of the Constitution, we have since departed
from the narrow view on which that decision rested. Indeed,
we have expressly held that the Fourth Amendment governs
not only the seizure of tangible items, but extends as well to
the recording of oral statements, over-heard without any
"technical trespass under . . . local property law" [*Silverman
v. United States*]. Once this much is acknowledged, and once
it is recognized that the Fourth Amendment protects people—
and not simply "areas"—against unreasonable searches and
seizures, it becomes clear that the reach of that Amendment
cannot turn upon the presence or absence of a physical intrusion into any given enclosure.

We conclude that the underpinnings of *Olmstead* and
Goldman have been so eroded by our subsequent decisions
that the "trespass" doctrine there enunciated can no longer
be regarded as controlling. The Government's activities in
electronically listening to and recording the petitioner's
words violated the privacy upon which he justifiably relied
while using the telephone booth and thus constituted a
"search and seizure" within the meaning of the Fourth
Amendment. The fact that the electronic device employed to
achieve that end did not happen to penetrate the wall of the
booth can have no constitutional significance.

A Warrantless Search and Seizure

The question remaining for decision, then, is whether the
search and seizure conducted in this case complied with constitutional standards. In that regard, the Government's position is that its agents acted in an entirely defensible manner:
They did not begin their electronic surveillance until investi-

gation of the petitioner's activities had established a strong probability that he was using the telephone in question to transmit gambling information to persons in other States, in violation of federal law. Moreover, the surveillance was limited, both in scope and in duration, to the specific purpose of establishing the contents of the petitioner's unlawful telephonic communications. The agents confirmed their surveillance to the brief periods during which he used the telephone booth, and they took great care to overhear only the conversations of the petitioner himself.

Accepting this account of the Government's actions as accurate, it is clear that this surveillance was so narrowly circumscribed that a duly authorized magistrate, properly notified of the need for such investigation, specifically informed of the basis on which it was to proceed, and clearly apprised of the precise intrusion it would entail, could constitutionally have authorized, with appropriate safeguards, the very limited search and seizure that the Government asserts in fact took place. Only last Term we sustained the validity of such an authorization, holding that, under sufficiently "precise and discriminate circumstances," a federal court may empower government agents to employ a concealed electronic device "for the narrow and particularized purpose of ascertaining the truth of the . . . allegations" of a "detailed factual affidavit alleging the commission of a specific criminal offense" [*Osborn v. United States*]. Discussing that holding, the Court in *Berger v. New York* said that "the order authorizing the use of the electronic device" in *Osborn* "afforded similar protections to those . . . of conventional warrants authorizing the seizure of tangible evidence." Through those protections, "no greater invasion of privacy was permitted than was necessary under the circumstances." Here, too, a similar judicial order could have accommodated "the legitimate needs of law enforcement" by authorizing the carefully limited use of electronic surveillance.

Governmental Restraint Is Not Enough

The Government urges that, because its agents relied upon the decisions in *Olmstead* and *Goldman*, and because they did no more here than they might properly have done with prior judicial sanction, we should retroactively validate their conduct. That we cannot do. It is apparent that the agents in this case acted with restraint. Yet the inescapable fact is that this restraint was imposed by the agents themselves, not by a judicial officer. They were not required, before commencing the search, to present their estimate of probable cause for detached scrutiny by a neutral magistrate. They were not compelled, during the conduct of the search itself, to observe precise limits established in advance by a specific court order. Nor were they directed, after the search had been completed, to notify the authorizing magistrate in detail of all that had been seized. In the absence of such safeguards, this Court has never sustained a search upon the sole ground that officers reasonably expected to find evidence of a particular crime and voluntarily confined their activities to the least intrusive means consistent with that end. Searches conducted without warrants have been held unlawful "notwithstanding facts unquestionably showing probable cause" [*Agnello v. United States*] for the Constitution requires "that the deliberate, impartial judgment of a judicial officer . . . be interposed between the citizen and the police . . ." [*Wong Sun v. United States*]. "Over and again this Court has emphasized that the mandate of the [Fourth] Amendment requires adherence to judicial processes" [*United States v. Jeffers*], and that searches conducted outside the judicial process, without prior approval by judge or magistrate, are per se unreasonable under the Fourth Amendment—subject only to a few specifically established and well-delineated exceptions.

It is difficult to imagine how any of those exceptions could ever apply to the sort of search and seizure involved in this case. Even electronic surveillance substantially contemporaneous with an individual's arrest could hardly be deemed an "incident" of that arrest. Nor could the use of electronic surveillance without prior authorization be justified on grounds of "hot pursuit." And, of course, the very nature of electronic surveillance precludes its use pursuant to the suspect's consent.

The Government does not question these basic principles. Rather, it urges the creation of a new exception to cover this case. It argues that surveillance of a telephone booth should be exempted from the usual requirement of advance authorization by a magistrate upon a showing of probable cause. We cannot agree. Omission of such authorization

> bypasses the safeguards provided by an objective pre-determination of probable cause, and substitutes instead the far less reliable procedure of an after-the-event justification for the . . . search, too likely to be subtly influenced by the familiar shortcomings of hindsight judgment [*Beck v. Ohio*].

And bypassing a neutral predetermination of the scope of a search leaves individuals secure from Fourth Amendment violations "only in the discretion of the police" [*Beck v. Ohio*].

The considerations do not vanish when the search in question is transferred from the setting of a home, an office, or a hotel room to that of a telephone booth. Wherever a man may be, he is entitled to know that he will remain free from unreasonable searches and seizures. The government agents here ignored "the procedure of antecedent justification . . . that is central to the Fourth Amendment" [*Osborn v. United States*], a procedure that we hold to be a constitutional precondition of the kind of electronic surveillance involved in this case. Because the surveillance here failed to meet that condition, and because it led to the petitioner's conviction, the judgment must be reversed.

The *Katz* Decision Changed the Application of the Fourth Amendment

Charles E. Moylan Jr.

In the following selection, Charles E. Moylan Jr., a former judge on the Maryland Court of Special Appeals, describes the Supreme Court's 1967 decision in *Katz v. United States* and its influence on how the Fourth Amendment is interpreted and applied. Moylan summarizes the majority opinion by Potter Stewart as well as a concurring opinion by John Marshall Harlan. These opinions, while agreeing that the Fourth Amendment protected people using a public telephone from unfair search and seizure, lent themselves to differing interpretations regarding the scope of Fourth Amendment protection. In addition, Harlan's argument that the Fourth Amendment applied whenever a person had a "reasonable expectation of privacy" changed the way scholars talked about applying the Fourth Amendment. Since the introduction of this phrase, according to Moylan, the Fourth Amendment has been applied with more flexibility.

The 1967 decision of *Katz v. United States* has arguably had a greater impact on the Fourth Amendment than any other single Supreme Court decision with the exception of *Mapp v. Ohio* (1961). Its impact, however, has been exclusively on the subject of threshold applicability or coverage. It may not have altered the substantive law with respect to coverage, but it has changed dramatically the vocabulary we use when we talk about coverage. The special impact of *Katz*, moreover, has proceeded not from the majority opin-

Charles E. Moylan Jr., *The Fourth Amendment Handbook: A Chronological Survey of Supreme Court Decisions.* Chicago: Criminal Justice Section, American Bar Association, 2003. Copyright © 2003 by the American Bar Association. All rights reserved. Reproduced by permission.

ion of the Court but from the concurring opinion of Justice [John Marshall] Harlan. That concurrence, however, has been cited and quoted with approval so regularly by subsequent decisions of the Supreme Court that it has ripened into the majority position.

The factual issue in *Katz* was a narrow one. FBI agents had warrantlessly placed an electronic eavesdropping device on the roof of a public telephone booth in Los Angeles, California. By the use of that "bug," they recorded the voice of Charles Katz as he illegally transmitted wagering information to contacts in Miami and Boston. There was no issue as to satisfaction of the Fourth Amendment for it was clear that the FBI agents, with ample time to have obtained a court order for the placement of the listening device, had not done so. If the Fourth Amendment applied, therefore, it had been violated. The only issue was that of whether the Fourth Amendment even covered the situation.

The earlier Supreme Court precedents of *Olmstead v. United States* (1928) and *Goldman v. United States* (1942) had held that there was no Fourth Amendment involvement unless there was a physical penetration into the constitutionally protected area. The electronic listening device at issue, like the one found to have been unoffending in *Goldman*, was one that did not penetrate the structure and did not, therefore, invade the constitutionally protected area. That distinction the Supreme Court repudiated, expressly overruling *Olmstead* and *Goldman* to the extent to which they had held a physical penetration into the constitutionally protected area the sine qua non of Fourth Amendment involvement. To do so, however, the Supreme Court had to change the way in which it described Fourth Amendment coverage.

The Broad Language of *Katz*

The *Katz* decision itself, confined to its factual context, was straightforward and free of confusion. The at-times-broad language of the *Katz* opinion, however, generated significant confusion and debate. Some argued that the very concept of a constitutionally protected perimeter was dead and that Fourth Amendment coverage had moved from inside that

traditional perimeter to the broad outside. The predicate for
that notion was the seven words early in the majority opinion, "the Fourth Amendment protects people, not places." Ar-
guing against a too hasty conclusion that the very concept of
"place" had lost its significance was the follow-up reference
in the majority opinion, two paragraphs after the first, in
which it stated, "the Fourth Amendment protects people—
and not *simply* 'areas'" (emphasis supplied). Justice Harlan's
concurrence, moreover, carefully pointed out:

> As the Court's opinion states, "the Fourth Amendment
> protects people, not places." The question, however, is
> what protection it affords to those people. Generally, as
> here, the answer to that question requires reference to a
> "place."

The opposite reading of the *Katz* decision in this regard
was that it had not moved Fourth Amendment coverage from
inside the traditionally protected area to the broad outside,
for those were not the facts of *Katz*, but that it had, rather,
enhanced the quality of the protection within the constitutionally protected perimeter. Justice Harlan's concurrence
pointed out that for the period of its use and occupancy "an
enclosed telephone booth is an area where, like a home," a
person enjoys Fourth Amendment protection and is "unlike a
field" where there is no such protection. That reading of *Katz*
was that within the protected telephone booth, the thing protected was the privacy of the person inside the place and
not the structural integrity of the "place" itself—the wood-
work, the stucco, the glass. That, it was argued, was the
intended meaning of protecting "people, not places." In repu-
diating *Olmstead* and *Goldman*, therefore, the Supreme
Court had ruled that it was protecting a person inside such a
protected area from such highly sophisticated intrusive, but
non-penetrating, devices as laser beams and parabolic micro-
phones and detecta-phones, just as traditionally it had protected against such old-fashioned penetrating devices as
jimmies and crowbars and spike-mikes.

The debate between the two positions posed the classic law
school issue of what is the law of the case when the decision

itself, on its facts, is narrow, but where the language of the opinion announcing the decision is broad. In 1984, the well-reasoned analysis of Justice [Lewis] Powell in *Oliver v. United States* [which ruled that there is no Fourth Amendment protection in open fields] settled the debate in favor of the narrower interpretation, pointing out that that was the only interpretation that had a base in the actual facts of the *Katz* case itself.

Impact of Harlan's Concurrence

The more far-reaching impact of *Katz* has stemmed from the concurring opinion of Justice Harlan. In groping for a way to describe Fourth Amendment coverage, he came up with the phrase "a reasonable expectation of privacy." It caught on. He broke it down into two component parts—its subjective aspect and its objective aspect. It is initially required that an individual have an actual or subjective expectation of privacy. Thus, even in the otherwise protected venue of a man's home, "objects, activities, or statements that he exposes to the 'plain view' of others are not 'protected' because no intention to keep them to himself has been exhibited." In the years since the *Katz* opinion was promulgated, emphasis has shifted decidedly away from this subjective aspect of a reasonable expectation of privacy and onto the objective aspect.

Even if an individual has an actual, subjective expectation of privacy, that does not translate into a Fourth Amendment protection unless such expectation is also one that society has objectively recognized as reasonable. "Conversations in the open would not be protected against being overheard for the expectation of privacy under the circumstances would be unreasonable [Cf. *Hester v. United States*]." It is because of the critical significance of this objective aspect of "a reasonable expectation of privacy" that the impact of *Katz* on the threshold issue of Fourth Amendment coverage is revealed to be more linguistic than substantive.

A Changed Amendment

Where one used to ask, "Did the defendant enjoy a Fourth Amendment protection?," one now asks, "Did the defendant possess a reasonable expectation of privacy?" These are two ways of saying precisely the same thing. A Fourth Amendment protection is defined as "a reasonable expectation of privacy." Either the Fourth Amendment protection directly or the objectively measured "reasonable expectation of privacy" are then determined by such traditional inquiries as

1. Was the place that was searched covered by the Fourth Amendment?
2. Was the searcher an agent of government?
3. Was it the defendant, and not someone else, who enjoyed the protection or the expectation and, therefore, has the standing to raise the question?
4. Was the type of police conduct in issue a "search" or "seizure" or was it something else not covered by the Fourth Amendment?

The net effect has been simply to move such traditional inquiries one step further down in the outline. What used to be

I. Was There a Fourth Amendment Protection?
   A. Coverage of Place
   B. Coverage of Searcher
   C. Coverage of Defendant
   D. Coverage of Type of Police Conduct

might have become

I. Was There a "Reasonable Expectation of Privacy"?
   A. Subjectively
   B. Objectively
      1. Coverage of Place
      2. Coverage of Searcher
      3. Coverage of Defendant
      4. Coverage of Type of Police Conduct

The most significant effect of the substitution of the new "reasonable expectation of privacy" language seems to be that instead of measuring coverage mechanistically—on an "all or nothing" basis—we measure it more flexibly according to the "totality of the circumstances."

The Supreme Court Has Fundamentally Misinterpreted the Fourth Amendment

Akhil Reed Amar

Much of the history of the Supreme Court's interpretation of the Fourth Amendment has concerned the proper use of warrants. With some specific exceptions, the Court requires a warrant for any police search or seizure of evidence. In the following excerpt, Akhil Reed Amar, a law professor at Yale University and a well-known constitutional scholar, questions this entire approach. According to Amar, the founders did not intend to require a warrant for every search. In fact, the founders opposed the use of search warrants except as an emergency measure. They believed warrants were so objectionable that they should only be issued after a showing of probable cause. A search conducted without a warrant was not automatically unconstitutional, Amar argues. A person who believed he or she had been subjected to an unfair search had the option of bringing a civil suit against the parties responsible.

Reflect, for a moment, on the fact that the Fourth Amendment actually contains two different commands. First, all government searches and seizures must be reasonable. Second, no warrants shall issue without probable cause. The modern Supreme Court has intentionally collapsed the two requirements, treating all unwarranted searches and seizures —with various exceptions, such as exigent circumstances— as per se unreasonable. Otherwise, the Court has reasoned, the requirement that a neutral magistrate verify probable cause ex ante [beforehand] would be obviously frustrated—

the special safeguards of the warrant clause would be all but meaningless.

If we assume that the amendment is primarily about protecting minority rights and further assume that judges and magistrates are the best institutional guardians of those rights, this reading might seem to make sense. Why should government officials be allowed greater latitude (general reasonableness rather than the stricter probable cause) when they intentionally avoid the courtroom and intrude on individuals in a judicially unwarranted manner? Hence the seeming need, under these assumptions, to engraft a constructive second sentence onto the amendment: "Absent special circumstances, no search or seizure shall occur without a warrant."

But the fact that the amendment does not contain such a sentence should invite us to rethink our assumptions. (So should the combination of the silliness of the engrafted sentence without the "special circumstances" escape hatch, and the extraordinary difficulty of specifying the appropriate size and shape of the hatch. Indeed, reading a warrant requirement into the amendment, and then reading an elaborate set of exceptions into that warrant requirement, seems more like rewriting the amendment than reading it as written.) To begin rethinking, consider the paradigmatic way in which Fourth Amendment rights were to be enforced at the Founding. Virtually any search or seizure by a federal officer would involve a physical trespass under common-law principles. An aggrieved target could use the common law of trespass to bring suit for damages against the official—just as Wilkes brought a trespass action in [*Wilkes v.*] *Wood*.[1] If the search or seizure were deemed lawful in court, the defendant would prevail; but if, as in *Wood*, the search were found unlawful, the defendant government official would be held strictly liable. There was no such thing as "good faith" immunity.

Given this risk, many officials would obviously prefer to litigate the lawfulness of a contemplated search or seizure

---

1. Eighteenth-century English radical John Wilkes successfully sued for the return of illegally seized papers in a famous 1763 case that inspired the Founders.

before it occurred—to seek a judicial warrant authorizing the intrusion. Such a warrant, if strictly complied with, would act as a sort of declaratory judgment whose preclusive effect could be subsequently pled in any later damage action. A lawful warrant, in effect, would compel a sort of directed verdict for the defendant government official in any subsequent lawsuit for damages.

Problems with Warrants

But note what has happened. A warrant issued by a judge or magistrate—a permanent government official, on the government payroll—has had the effect of taking a later trespass action away from a jury of ordinary citizens. Because juries could often be trusted more than judges to protect against government overreaching . . . warrants were generally *dis*favored: "*No* warrants shall issue, but . . . ." And warrants had other flaws. First, they issued from a single person (as opposed to a judge sitting alongside a jury, twelve good men and true). Next, that single decisionmaker was an officer of the central government (unlike jurors of the community). Also, the decision occurred ex parte [by one party only], with no notice or opportunity to be heard given to the target of a search. Moreover, the warrant proceeding was a secret affair, unlike a tort suit open to the watchful eye of a public able to monitor its judicial agents. . . . Thus even when issued by a judge— and in some places executive magistrates also claimed authority to issue warrants—warrants lacked many traditional safeguards of judicial process: notice, adversarial presentation of issues, publicity, and so on. To make matters even worse, the government could forum shop; if only a single magistrate were lazy or abusive, cynical officers would know where to go to get an easy warrant. Judges and warrants are the heavies, not the heroes, of our story.

Warrantless Searches Acceptable

We can now see the Fourth Amendment with fresh eyes. Searches without warrants are not presumptively illegitimate; nor does every warrantless search or seizure require probable cause. Rather, whenever such a search or seizure occurred, a jury, guided by a judge in a public trial and able to hear arguments from both sides of the case, could typically assess the reasonableness of government action in an after-the-fact tort suit. If the properly instructed jury deemed the search unreasonable, the plain words of the Fourth Amendment would render the search unlawful. The defendant official could thus be held strictly liable and made to pay compensatory and (in egregious cases) punitive damages (though he might well in turn be indemnified by the government). The ultimate issue—were the defendant's actions reasonable or unreasonable—was often a classic question of fact for the jury; and the Seventh Amendment, in combination with the Fourth, would require the federal government to furnish a jury to any plaintiff-victim who demanded one and to protect that jury's finding of fact from being overturned by any judge or other government official. The prospect of jury oversight and jury-awarded punitive damages would powerfully deter government officials contemplating unreasonable conduct. (In England, the government ended up paying out a king's ransom in damages and court expenses in the Wilkes affair.) Judicial warrants, though, were another matter. Precisely because they were granted by government officials in closed ex parte proceedings—and had the effect of taking the reasonableness issue away from the jury altogether—they had to be strictly limited. Such warrants needed to meet stricter requirements (probable cause, and so on) than mere reasonableness.

Thus, contrary to the modern Court's approach, the words of the Fourth Amendment mean what they say: warrantless searches are not always unconstitutional, and the probable-cause requirement applies only if and when a warrant issues. Put another way, the Court has simply misread the original linkage between the Fourth Amendment's two different commands. It is not that a search or seizure without a warrant was presumptively unreasonable, as the Court has assumed; rather, an overbroad warrant lacking probable cause or specificity—in other words, a general warrant—was per se unreasonable, in part because it unjustifiably displaced the proper role of the jury. . . .

Warrants as Emergency Measures

If warrants were in some ways like prior restraints, why, it might be asked, didn't the framers of the Fourth Amendment simply ban all warrants? A good modern-day analogy is the temporary restraining order. Sometimes, emergency action must be taken to freeze the status quo and prevent future harm, and so judges may act ex parte, without the traditional safeguards of adversarial adjudication. But precisely because of the due-process dangers it poses, an ex parte temporary restraining order is strictly limited to situations where there is a risk of "irreparable injury" and a high likelihood of "success on the merits." At common law, a warrant could likewise issue when there was a high likelihood—"probable cause"—that a particular place contained stolen goods. The whole point of the ex parte warrant was to authorize a search that would bring the stolen goods before the magistrate. To give the owner of the hideaway a heads-up in advance of the surprise search might enable him to whisk the goods away—a kind of irreparable injury to the truth, to the justice system, and to the victim of the theft seeking to recover his goods. The need for a surprise search on these facts is obviously strong, but without the absolute guarantee of immunity provided by a warrant, an officer might hesitate to perform the surprise search for fear of a future lawsuit. Once extended beyond the limited context of the common-law warrant for stolen goods, though, warrants had the potential for great evil. If general warrants were authorized on less than probable cause, they would give government henchmen absolute power to "round up the usual suspects," rousting political enemies (like Wilkes). In the end, the Fourth Amendment framers accepted some warrants as necessary but imposed strict limits on these dangerous devices. Warrantless searches did not pose the same threat because those searches would be subject to full and open after-the-fact review in civil-trespass cases featuring civil juries.

CHAPTER THREE

Current Perspectives on Search and Seizure

The Bill of Rights

The Fourth Amendment Limits Schools' Powers to Search Students

Benjamin Dowling-Sendor

The courts have traditionally given schools considerably greater latitude than they have law enforcement officers in conducting searches, even random searches, of students. In two major cases, the Supreme Court has upheld the right of schools to conduct drug tests of athletes and of other students participating in competitive extracurricular activities. Some schools have gone further and conducted random searches of students. In the following article, Benjamin Dowling-Sendor, an assistant appellate defender and an expert in school law, describes a case in which the Eighth U.S. Circuit Court of Appeals found a random search of students unconstitutional. When school officials in Little Rock, Arkansas, ordered all students to empty out pockets, bookbags, and other belongings for inspection, they found marijuana on one student, who was convicted of possession. The student appealed, and the Eighth Circuit Court found that such a sweeping search did violate her Fourth Amendment protections. In agreeing with the court's decision, Dowling-Sendor notes that searches should have some reasonable relationship to a clear and definite danger. Both school officials and students should be aware that despite their greater latitude, schools cannot simply ride roughshod over their students' Fourth Amendment rights.

It was only a matter of time. At some point after the U.S. Supreme Court upheld random drug testing for athletes

(*Vernonia School District 47J v. Acton* [1995]) and for students who participate in any competitive extracurricular activities (*Board of Education of Independent School District No. 92 of Pottawatomie County v. Earls* [2002]), a court somewhere in America was going to consider the constitutionality of random searches of *all* students.

A recent decision by the 8th U.S. Circuit Court of Appeals, *Doe ex rel. Doe v. Little Rock School District*, tackles this issue.

The Facts in the Case

Jane Doe—or so she was called in the case—was a high school student in Little Rock, Ark., in 1999–2000. The district had a practice of conducting random searches of secondary school students' belongings.

The student handbook states that "book bags, backpacks, purses, and similar containers are permitted on school property as a convenience for students" but that once they are on school property, "such containers are at all times subject to random and periodic inspections by school officials." Any contraband that is discovered is given to law enforcement agencies as evidence to use in criminal prosecutions against offending students.

One day, according to the opinion of the 8th Circuit, all students in Jane's class were directed to empty their pockets, put all of their belongings (including backpacks and purses) on their desks, and leave the classroom. While the students stood outside in the hall, school employees searched the items on their desks.

A search of Jane's purse revealed a container with marijuana. The marijuana was turned over to law enforcement officers, and Jane was convicted of a misdemeanor drug offense.

Jane sued the school district in U.S. District Court, contending that the practice of conducting random searches violated the Fourth Amendment's prohibition against unreasonable searches and seizures.

After the District Court dismissed Jane's suit, she appealed to the 8th Circuit. In a 2-1 decision, the 8th Circuit reversed the District Court ruling and agreed with Jane that the practice violates the Fourth Amendment.

A Progression of Case Law

Writing for the court, Judge Morris Sheppard Arnold traced the law governing student searches back to the Supreme Court's 1985 decision in *New Jersey v. T.L.O.* In that seminal case, the Supreme Court ruled that the Fourth Amendment's prohibition against unreasonable searches and seizures applies to school searches.

However, the high court also ruled that the usual requirements for searches by law enforcement officers—probable cause to believe that a search will reveal contraband or evidence of a crime and, in some cases, a search warrant—do not apply to searches of students by school employees.

The court applied a more lenient standard to student searches: The Fourth Amendment permits such searches as long as they are reasonable in both their inception and their scope. The court ruled that the Fourth Amendment allows such searches if school employees have a reasonable, articulable suspicion that the search will reveal contraband or evidence of a crime or a violation of school rules.

Although *T.L.O.* gave school officials substantial leeway in deciding whether and how to conduct student searches, the case still put some constraints on them. But then even these mild limits on student searches ran into the problem of student drug use.

In 1995, in *Vernonia*, the Supreme Court upheld random urinalysis for student athletes after the school district presented evidence that athletes played a key role in the district's drug culture. Then, in 2002, in *Earls*, the court extended the scope of *Vernonia* by upholding random urinalysis for students involved in any competitive extracurricular activities.

It was inevitable that the next question would be the constitutionality of random searches (whether urinalysis or other kinds of searches) of all students.

Judge Arnold studied *T.L.O.*, *Vernonia*, and *Earls* to guide his analysis in this case. As Arnold explained, the Supreme Court has identified four factors to balance the privacy interests of students with the security interests of school districts: (1) the scope of a student's legitimate expectation of privacy, (2) the nature of the intrusion caused by a search, (3) the nature and urgency of the school district's security concern, and (4) the effectiveness of a search as a means to address the security concern.

Arnold addressed the last three factors in this case.

Expectation of Privacy

A school district's duty to maintain discipline, health, and safety limits students' legitimate expectation of privacy during school activities, but students' privacy interests "are not nonexistent," Judge Arnold said. "We think it is clear that schoolchildren are entitled to expect some degree of privacy in the personal items that they bring to school."

Specifically, the Fourth Amendment protects, to some extent, the owner of any container whose contents are hidden from plain view. Accordingly, Arnold observed, the Fourth Amendment protects students from unreasonable searches of the variety of containers they bring to school, such as backpacks, purses, and the pockets of jackets and pants.

Quoting from *T.L.O.*, Arnold pointed out since compulsory attendance laws transform schools into "homes away from home" for a number of hours each weekday, students "at a minimum must bring to school not only the supplies needed for their studies, but also keys, money, and the necessities of personal hygiene and grooming," and they may also carry with them "such nondisruptive yet highly personal items as photographs, letters, and diaries."

Citing *Vernonia* and *Earls*, Judge Arnold acknowledged that the legitimate privacy expectations of some segments of the student body are less than "the already limited baseline level of privacy afforded to public school students generally."

For example, in *Vernonia*, the Supreme Court explained that the special rules of school sports teams—such as required physical exams, communal undress in locker rooms, and team travel—necessarily and reasonably intrude on the privacy of student athletes. Moreover, students implicitly accept those intrusions when they try out for athletic teams.

But the rationales for the reduced privacy of athletes don't apply to all students. As Arnold observed, "The search regime at issue here is imposed on the entire student body, so the [school district] cannot reasonably claim that those subject to search have made a voluntary tradeoff of some of their privacy interests in exchange for a benefit or privilege."

Judge Arnold rejected the school district's argument that in light of the notice about searches in the student handbook, students waive their privacy interests in the property they bring to school. In contrast to participation in sports teams and extracurricular activities, students are required by law to attend school. Students don't voluntarily choose to accept the provisions of the student handbook by complying with compulsory attendance laws. The school district, Arnold explained, "may not deprive its students of privacy expectations protected by the Fourth Amendment simply by announcing that the expectations will no longer be honored."

The Nature of the Intrusion

Turning to the character of the intrusion, Judge Arnold noted that in *T.L.O.*, the Supreme Court found that "[a] search of a child's purse or bag carried on her person, no less than a similar search carried out on an adult, is undoubtedly a severe violation of subjective expectations of privacy."

As Arnold pointed out, students often carry personal items in pockets and bags, "and many students (whether or not they are carrying contraband) must surely feel uncomfortable or embarrassed when officials decide to rifle through their personal belongings."

Arnold contrasted the full-scale searches at issue in this case with less-intrusive searches, such as dog sniffs and the use of metal detectors. He concluded that the type of search being challenged "is highly intrusive, and we are not aware of any cases indicated that such searches in schools pass constitutional muster absent individualized suspicion, consent or waiver of privacy interests by those searched, or extenuating circumstances that pose a grave security threat."

Arnold also emphasized that while the urinalysis results at issue in *Vernonia* and *Earls* were not disclosed to law enforcement agencies and led at most to exclusion from extracurricular activities, "the fruits of the searches at issue here are apparently regularly turned over to law enforcement officials and are used in criminal proceedings against students whose contraband is discovered. . . . Because the [district's] searches can lead directly to the imposition of punitive sanctions, the character of the intrusions is qualitatively more severe than that in *Vernonia* and *Earls*."

The Concern for Security

Finally, Judge Arnold considered the nature and urgency of the school district's concerns that led to the random searches. He noted that while the district had "expressed some generalized concerns about the existence of weapons and drugs in its schools, it conceded . . . that there is nothing in the record regarding the magnitude of any problems with weapons or drugs that it has actually experienced."

He pointed out that in contrast to the school districts in *Vernonia* and *Earls*, the Little Rock School District had not shown any evidence of "significant and immediate difficulties sufficient to give rise to a special need for such an unprecedented practice."

Arnold also contrasted this case with the 1996 case decided by the 8th Circuit, *Thompson v. Carthage School District*. In *Thompson*, the court upheld a search of all male students in grades six through 12 for knives and guns because of "fresh cuts" on the seats of a school bus one morning and reports of a gun at school the same morning. That evidence "provided particularized evidence that there were dangerous weapons present on school grounds" that day.

"The mere assertion," Judge Arnold concluded, "that there are substantial problems associated with drugs and weapons in its schools does not give the [district] *carte blanche* to inflict highly intrusive, random searches upon its general student body."

Suspicion vs. Speculation

Judge C. Arlen Beam partly agreed with and partly dissented from Judge Arnold's majority opinion. He agreed with Arnold that the use of the fruits of student searches by the police to prosecute students was troubling. However, in Beam's view, the general problems with drugs and weapons in schools around the country gave the school district a strong enough interest to justify random searches of all students.

Beam also noted evidence that since the implementation of the search policy, the school district had disciplined students for bringing weapons as small as razor blades to school and that incidents had occurred in which students had tried to use razor blades as weapons.

Although I recognize the problems of student possession of drugs and weapons, I side with Judge Arnold. The severity of such problems in some school districts does not by itself justify a policy calling for random intrusive searches of all students in another school district.

Searches for drugs or weapons in one district can be justified only by evidence of a significant problem involving student possession of drugs or weapons in that district. Even though there was evidence that an unspecified number of weapons had been found since the search policy began, there still was no evidence of a serious, urgent, general problem with the possession of weapons or drugs in the school district.

Are there circumstances that would justify random searches of an entire student body? I think the answer is yes. For example, if evidence showed a serious, widespread problem of drug possession by all segments of a school's student body, a random search policy (possibly even a random urinalysis policy) might be legally justified. And as the 8th Circuit's own decision in *Thompson* shows, reasonable suspicion (not mere speculation) about student possession of weapons—especially of firearms—might well justify a search of an entire student body.

But, as Judge Arnold observed, there was no evidence of such problems in this case.

New Technologies Create New Threats to Privacy Rights

Jeffrey Rosen

Traditionally, the Fourth Amendment has been interpreted as protecting people's right against unreasonable searches on private property. However, as Jeffrey Rosen, a legal affairs expert at the *New Republic* magazine, explains in the following excerpt, the creation of large computer databases containing personal information poses a new threat to privacy. So-called mass dataveillance involves searching the computer records of millions of innocent people to find possible suspects, or simply suspicious behavior. Because this information is compiled and kept by private third parties, such as banks, libraries, and hospitals, it is currently outside the scope of Fourth Amendment protection. Rosen argues that Congress is more likely than the courts to protect Americans against government abuses resulting from dataveillance, but he fears that the public will oppose such efforts.

Constitutional doctrine, as it has evolved, provides remarkably few restrictions on surveillance technologies that threaten privacy and freedom without protecting security, which makes the need for congressional oversight especially acute. Consider the constitutional dangers posed by mass dataveillance, which occurs when the government searches the private data of millions of innocent citizens in the hope of identifying suspicious patterns. Although Congress rejected the Total Information Awareness data-mining project in its original form, other models of mass dataveillance—such as the advanced Computer Assisted Passenger

Jeffrey Rosen, *The Naked Crowd: Reclaiming Security and Freedom in an Anxious Age.* New York: Random House, 2004. Copyright © 2004 by Jeffrey Rosen. All rights reserved. Reproduced by permission of the publisher.

Screening system—are now being implemented at airports around the world. To guard against broad fishing expeditions, the courts could, in theory, hold that the Fourth Amendment to the Constitution prohibits the government using mass dataveillance to search for evidence of low-level wrongdoing and to prosecute citizens for crimes unrelated to terrorism. Judges in the eighteenth century, after all, ruled that the most invasive searches should be limited to the most dangerous crimes: A private diary, for example, might be seized in connection with a murder investigation but not to prove seditious libel against the Crown. During the twentieth century, however, judges stopped demanding a degree of proportionality between the intrusiveness of a search and the seriousness of a suspected crime. As a result, courts today are not likely to save us from the excesses of personal dataveillance.

This conclusion might seem surprising. Unlike the Carnivore e-mail search program, which targets only suspicious information, mass dataveillance allows the government to search a great deal of innocent information. When the government engages in mass dataveillance to conduct general searches of millions of citizens without cause to believe that a crime has been committed, the searches arguably raise the same dangers in the twenty-first century as the general warrants that the framers of the Fourth Amendment feared in the eighteenth century. Dataveillance, like a general warrant, gives the government essentially unlimited discretion to search through masses of personal information in search of suspicious activity, without specifying in advance the people, places, or things it expects to find. Both general warrants and dataveillance allow fishing expeditions in which the government is trolling for crimes rather than particular criminals, violating the privacy of millions of innocent people in the hope of finding a handful of unknown and unidentified terrorists.

And yet American constitutional law, as it has developed, says that general warrants are unconstitutional, while dataveillance, in most circumstances, is perfectly legal. This jarring conclusion results from the fact that our law of unreasonable searches and seizures originally relied on conceptions of private property to protect privacy. If a search invaded a protected space, like the home, then it was presumptively unreasonable. But once personal information, such as diaries, financial data, letters, and health-care information, began to be stored outside the home, in electronic databases, judges struggled in vain to protect it from general searches by the government. In a series of cases in the 1970s and 1980s, the Supreme Court held that citizens have no reasonable expectation of privacy in information that they have turned over to third parties, such as bank records and telephone dialing information. Although dataveillance, in some ways, reveals even more personal information to the state than a general warrant does, our courts have refused to recognize dataveillance as a search at all, merely because it takes place outside the home.

American courts have been similarly slow to recognize the threat to privacy posed by systems of ubiquitous surveillance in public. The test of whether an unreasonable search has occurred, the Court held in the 1960s, was whether an individual has a subjective expectation of privacy that society is prepared to accept as reasonable. Although initially hailed as a victory for privacy, it soon became clear that this test was circular. People's subjective expectations of privacy reflect the privacy they subjectively experience, and as electronic surveillance in public became more intrusive and more pervasive, it lowered people's objective expectation of privacy as well, with a corresponding diminution of constitutional protections. Following this circular logic, the Court held in the 1970s and 1980s that people have little objective expectation of privacy in public places, even when their movements are observed by technologically enhanced searches (such as helicopters flying over the backyard), because all of us have to assume the risk that our movements in public might be observed. Carried to its logical conclusion, this reasoning would eviscerate privacy by allowing the government to place a camera on each citizen's shoulder to track all of his or her movements in public. This is the characteristic of a police state, not a free society; but the Court seemed unable to distinguish between the risk that a stranger might observe us in passing and the risk that the government might bug us twenty-four hours a day.

The federal government is currently prohibited from centralizing and analyzing large amounts of personal data, but these legal restrictions often don't apply to the analysis of data that are stored in private databases. The government, as a result, has access to increasing amounts of personal information that has been legally collected by commercial data warehouses such as ChoicePoint, which specializes in sorting and packaging more than 10 billion records, indexed by social security number, that have been obtained from marketers, private detectives, and credit card bureaus. From private corporations, state agents can obtain our telephone records, bank records, cable TV records, and credit card records. From our employers and Internet service providers, they can obtain the e-mail we send and the Internet addresses we browse. From credit card reporting agencies, they can obtain detailed reports about our opinions, buying habits, reading habits, and medical prescriptions. After 9/11, this trend increased, as the FBI, without a subpoena or court order, requested records from businesses; companies that had previously been concerned about appearing to violate the privacy of their customers turned over the information without complaint. In the wake of the terrorist attacks, several large financial companies agreed to turn over information to the FBI.

Mass dataveillance, as I suggested in the prologue, poses at least three distinct dangers: It creates a danger of unlimited bureaucratic discretion, encouraging officials to troll for low-level crimes. The British experience with CCTV shows the danger of a snooping society, in which state officials use the threat of terrorism as a pretext for maintaining constant surveillance of society as a whole. It makes it hard for individuals to clear their names or escape their past. And it is a technology of classification and exclusion that limits people's opportunities based on their perceived trustworthiness. But according to the courts, these dangers, however troubling, do not rise to the level of violating constitutional rights. Let's consider each of these three dangers in turn.

First, there is the danger of unsupervised discretion when state agents are free to scan a great deal of innocent activity and then prosecute people for low-level crimes. . . . Trolling for low-level forms of social disorder allows state officers to reserve for themselves the power to pick individuals out of the crowd and to punish them for relatively minor crimes that would otherwise go unpunished. Although this sort of ubiquitous surveillance is associated in totalitarian societies with Big Brotherism, it's perhaps more accurate, in societies that have traditionally been suspicious of centralized authority, such as England and America, to worry more about the costs of unchecked bureaucratic discretion. In a society in which all personal data are transparent, and many forms of low-level disorder are illegal, state authorities have tremendous discretion to pick and choose among offenses and offenders.

The danger of giving the police unlimited discretion to troll for low-level crimes that can then be linked to certain individuals or groups is, of course, the basic objection to racial profiling. As William Stuntz has argued, racial profiling on the highways of America is essentially unregulated because of two related developments in the law of unreasonable searches and seizures. First, the Supreme Court has said that the police can arrest a citizen who is guilty of any crime, even a very trivial crime. The leading case is *Atwater v. City of Lago Vista*, where the Court rejected the claim that driving without a seat belt was too minor an infraction to justify hauling a suburban mother off to the police station in handcuffs. Second, the Court has said that as long as an officer has the legal authority to search and seize a citizen, his or her actual motive for doing so is irrelevant. In *Whren v. United States*, the Court held that the police permissibly stopped two black teenagers for turning without signaling; it didn't matter that the police used the traffic stop as a pretext for allowing them to search for drugs. "Taken together, *Atwater* and *Whren* allow police officers to use trivial 'crimes' like minor traffic violations as an excuse to detain and search people whom they suspect of more serious offenses," Stuntz writes. "In legal terms, the debate about racial profiling on the highways is largely a debate about the merits of these

two rules. With them, officers can select a few speed-limit violators out of the large universe of such violators (all drivers
speed) and stop them in order to search for drugs—and that
course of action is perfectly legal. Without this pair of rules,
such behavior would be a great deal harder to justify."

Before 9/11, both of these legal rules were controversial.
Racial profiling of African American drivers in an effort to
find drugs seemed so unfair—its benefits so minor and its social costs so high—that even John Ashcroft, the Republican
attorney general, promised to eradicate the practice in America. Moreover, the Supreme Court's 5-4 *Atwater* decision,
which held that the intrusiveness of a search or seizure need
not have any relation to the seriousness of the crime being
investigated, was remarkably unconvincing. In his opinion
for the Court, Justice David Souter claimed that in the eighteenth century, officers could arrest anyone they had probable cause to believe had committed a crime, no matter how
minor. Souter's historical claims were dubious, and there is a
strong argument that the historical evidence actually sup-
ports the opposite conclusion: In the eighteenth century, arrests without a warrant for minor offenses were generally
unlawful, except in some well-defined categories of minor offenses where there was an unusual need for a prompt arrest.
The eighteenth-century framers were so concerned about executive discretion, in other words, that they insisted on limiting the most intrusive searches and seizures to the most
serious crimes. But after 9/11, the increased sympathy for
law enforcement makes it even less likely that judges will insist on resurrecting constitutional limits on executive discretion to search and seize.

The second danger that dataveillance presents is the danger that individuals will find it harder to escape their past in
a world of permanent and increasingly transparent data mining and profiling, like the low-level shoplifters who could set
off biometric alerts when they tried to enter the British Bor-
ders bookstore. But the courts have suggested that the Constitution provides no remedy for that harm, either. A citizen
who has been permanently flagged in a secret database has
been branded, in a sense, as infamous. But courts are not

likely to help the stigmatized individuals clear their names. The constitutional guarantee of "equal protection of the laws" has been interpreted to forbid the state from intentionally discriminating against citizens based on immutable characteristics, such as race or gender; but the personal information in a data profile is based on our past behavior rather than our immutable attributes, on what we have done rather than who we are.

Perhaps the closest analogies to an intrusive computer profile or system of dataveillance are the Internet sex crime registries that every state in the Union adopted after the murder of a child named Megan Kanka in 1994. The laws, ostensibly designed to protect public safety, typically require all sex offenders, both violent and nonviolent, to enroll in a public registry that is on the Internet. In 2003, the Supreme Court rejected constitutional challenges to Megan's Law in Alaska and Connecticut filed by two convicts who insisted that the government had unfairly tarred them as dangerous sex offenders without giving them a chance to prove that, in fact, they posed no threat to the community. An earlier ruling from 1976 had upheld a decision by a local police department to circulate to local merchants flyers displaying photographs of "active shoplifters." Although the police department had indeed stigmatized the shoplifters, Justice William Rehnquist held, they weren't deprived of any legally protected rights, such as the right to buy alcohol or to travel. In the same spirit, the Court held that the convicted sex offenders publicized on an Internet database, like former shoplifters, may have been stigmatized, but they were not deprived of any legal rights. As Justice Ruth Bader Ginsburg noted in a dissenting opinion, however, the man who was identified as a former sex offender on the Internet had experienced the indignity of having negative information published about himself without any opportunity to put himself in context by posting positive information, such as the fact that a lower court had granted him custody of his young daughter on the grounds that he had been rehabilitated after serving his time. The court found that he had a "very low risk of reoffending" and "is not a pedophile." But these highly relevant facts were omitted on the Internet sex registry, which lumped him together with far more dangerous characters.

Like an Internet sex offenders registry, a data-profiling system that flags former shoplifters or former deadbeat dads every time they try to board a plane arguably stigmatizes them without punishing them. Although the shoplifters would be embarrassed every time they were singled out for special searches, as long as they weren't prohibited from boarding the plane or entering the building, courts might well conclude that they weren't deprived of legal rights by the disclosure of truthful information. Nevertheless, it's hard not to have sympathy for the former shoplifters or former deadbeat dads who have been unfairly stigmatized by the state for low-level crimes long after their debt to society has been discharged. A "stigma" is a "mark or token of infamy, disgrace, or reproach," and a profiling system that made it impossible for Americans to escape from their past misdeeds could clearly stigmatize them in ways disproportionate to their original offenses.

The courts are also unlikely to provide a remedy for the third and final harm caused by dataveillance: discriminatory classification of citizens based on electronic profiles. To the degree that dataveillance leads to what [author] David Lyon calls "digital discrimination," it is not likely to be the kind of intentional discrimination that violates the Constitution. Risk profiles are based on a broad array of personal characteristics, and only a handful of them—race or religion, for example—are constitutionally suspicious. And courts have held repeatedly that as long as race or religion is only one factor in a broad profile that includes constitutionally unobjectionable data as well—such as financial information and travel destination—then the profile doesn't violate the Constitution. The fact that the discriminatory effects of risk profiles may be far more sweeping than those of racial profiling probably reduces their constitutional vulnerability: If everyone is sorted into risk categories, targeted citizens can't object that they are being singled out for special discrimination. . . .

As we will see in the epilogue, it's possible to imagine various models for technological and legal oversight of the most extreme and invasive forms of surveillance, data mining, and profiling. I've argued that congressional oversight, subject to political accountability, offers the most promising avenue for regulation: Despite the polarized nature of the legislative debate, Congress has proved more willing than the courts to balance the executive's demand for security above all against more moderate alternatives. But architectures that protect liberty and security can't be imposed on the public against its will; in order to strike a reasonable balance between privacy and security, the public would have to care about privacy in a sustainable way, and it's not clear that we really do. We expose details of our personal lives on talk shows and on the Internet, and we enjoy watching others expose themselves in a similarly exhibitionistic way on reality TV. Far from trying to master our fears, we wallow in them by watching TV shows like *Fear Factor*, where participants are forced to reenact their most dreaded anxieties; and we crave similar alarmism from cable TV news, which has become like a 24/7 version of a reality show, pandering fear as a form of voyeuristic entertainment.

When people say they care about privacy, in short, what they really mean is that they want control over the conditions of their personal exposure; and what they really fear isn't loss of privacy but loss of control. Americans are perfectly happy to violate their own privacy, and those of strangers, as long as they have an illusion of control over the conditions under which the violation occurs. As we will see in the next chapter, the same people who say they are concerned about having their privacy violated by the state are all too willing to expose personal information in exchange for an elusive and fleeting feeling of security and emotional connection. Given this unfortunate dynamic, in which the crowd demands exposure and individuals are happy to oblige, it seems unrealistic to expect that citizens will demand protections for the privacy of others when they perceive an immediate security benefit for themselves. A society of anxious exhibitionists who fear loss of control above all will choose security over privacy every time.

The Patriot Act Threatens Fourth Amendment Rights

Samuel Dash

In the wake of the terrorist attacks of September 11, 2001, Congress passed the Patriot Act, which greatly expanded the powers of intelligence agencies to search for suspects. In the following selection, Samuel Dash argues that the Patriot Act poses a serious threat to Fourth Amendment rights. Under the act, officials can conduct wiretaps without showing probable cause and can search homes without prior warning. Dash concludes that in addition to these Fourth Amendment protections, various other constitutional rights have been undermined in America's war on terror, including due process and freedom of assembly.

Dash was a professor of law at Georgetown University prior to his death in 2004.

After 9/11, the president and his attorney general demanded greater search and seizure powers than a permissive Supreme Court had already given them. Though members of Congress grumbled, they submitted to these demands, desiring to appear as patriotic as the president in the war on terrorism. They enacted and the president signed Public Law 107–56, entitled the "Uniting and Strengthening America by Providing Appropriate Tools Required to Intercept and Obstruct Terrorism Act." The words of this awkward title were carefully put together to create a dissent-chilling acronym: the USA-PATRIOT Act.

The USA-PATRIOT Act dangerously eliminates a number of limitations Congress had previously placed on government

Samuel Dash, *The Intruders: Unreasonable Searches and Seizures from King John to John Ashcroft.* New Brunswick, NJ: Rutgers University Press, 2004. Copyright © 2004 by Samuel Dash. All rights reserved. Reproduced by permission of the publisher.

surveillance of individuals, even in national security matters. Prior to 9/11, the Foreign Intelligence Surveillance Act, which permitted wiretapping and other forms of surveillance without the government having to show probable cause, was restricted to investigation of foreign spies. This broader power of surveillance was prohibited from use against American citizens, who were guaranteed the constitutional protections of the Fourth Amendment.

Under the new antiterror legislation, U.S. citizens lose their constitutional protection whenever federal law enforcement agents tell a federal judge that their investigation is relevant to foreign intelligence. The agents can then receive authority to wiretap the telephones of Americans and search their homes without having to comply with Fourth Amendment requirements of probable cause or particularly describing the thing or conversation to be seized or the place to be searched.

No Prior Notice

Worse yet, under this legislation, federal agents can sneak into the homes of Americans to obtain evidence without having to comply with the constitutional requirement of giving prior notice to the residents. All they have to do is tell the judge that giving notice would "impede their investigation." In ordinary criminal investigations, the Supreme Court has held that, under the Fourth Amendment, an officer with a warrant seeking to enter a home must first knock and announce his purpose, unless such notice would endanger the officer or lead to the imminent destruction of evidence. This requirement of notice is hallowed in ancient English law, which [legal scholar] Sir Edward Coke, in the seventeenth century, claimed derived from the Magna Carta.

In addition, the Bush administration succeeded in getting Congress to give federal agents authority to engage in dragnet wiretapping and searches. Under prior law, the agent had to be able to specify a particular target person or telephone. In the war on terrorism, the government complained that they could not always do so. Under the USA-PATRIOT Act, federal agents can now obtain roving warrants, good for any suspected person, place, or telephone anywhere in the country.

Undermining Attorney-Client Privilege

Attorney General John Ashcroft's appetite for increased investigative power was not satisfied by what Congress gave him in the USA-PATRIOT Act. Alarming the public by his predictions of new terrorist attacks and decrying the impediments he claimed law enforcement agents confronted under existing legal restrictions, the attorney general set about giving himself additional powers without benefit of legislation. Ashcroft issued a federal regulation authorizing prison officials to intercept and record telephone conversations between detainees in custody on suspicion of terrorism and their lawyers without prior judicial authority.

While the courts have permitted the monitoring of general prisoner phone calls on the ground that prisoners can have no reasonable expectation of privacy during such calls, they have prohibited the monitoring of prisoner communications with lawyers. These communications are protected by the Fourth Amendment and the attorney-client privilege. In reply to the American Bar Association's challenge to his actions, the attorney general explained that such recordings of attorney-client communications would only be made in a very few cases, and that he personally should be trusted to not misuse this power.

Uncontrolled Government Power

The fundamental principle upon which our constitutional protections are based is that powerful government officials cannot be so trusted. This concept is embodied in the oft-repeated statement of American judges that we are a government of law, not of men. James Madison illustrated this principle when he stated the following in *Federalist Papers 51*:

> If men were angels, no government would be necessary. If angels were to govern men, neither external or internal controls on government would be necessary. In framing a government which is to be administered by men over men, the great difficulty lies in this: you must first enable the government to control the governed; and in the next place to oblige it to control itself. A

dependence on the people is no doubt the primary control on the government; but experience has taught mankind the necessity of auxiliary precautions.

An example of such uncontrolled government power occurred shortly after terrorists, who were Arabs, crashed their hijacked airliners into the World Trade Center, the Pentagon, and the Pennsylvania countryside. Federal agents arrested and imprisoned more than one thousand Arab and South Asian immigrants. These arrests were based on minor immigration violations, such as expired visas. The government defended imprisoning these terrorist-looking foreign men on the ground that they might be involved in terrorism or were material witnesses. The attorney general refused to identify these detainees or allow them to have open hearings.

In addition, more than five thousand legal Muslim immigrants, many of whom were students in U.S. universities, were notified that they would be interrogated by FBI agents. Although these interrogations were supposed to be voluntary, the agents were not told to inform the immigrants that they could refuse to be questioned without fear of retaliation. Most of the immigrants believed that they had to undergo interrogation or suffer some kind of punishment. The Muslim community in the United States was frightened, embittered, and discouraged by the government's associating them with terrorism simply because of their appearance and religion. It was reminiscent of the internment of Japanese Americans after the attack on Pearl Harbor.

Racial Profiling

This type of law enforcement racial profiling had outraged Americans in the past. Prior to 9/11, the victims of this treatment were mostly African Americans and Latino Americans. The crime of "driving while black" had become all too common on the highways of the United States. Law enforcement officers had been criticized for such practices, and government leaders had promised to put a stop to them.

Law enforcement racial profiling began with an effort by the Supreme Court to accommodate a bona fide law enforcement need. In 1968, the Supreme Court was asked by the state of Ohio, and the many other states that joined in the case, to authorize police to briefly stop and frisk persons on the street on the basis of the lesser standard of suspicion rather than probable cause, which controlled regular arrests and searches. The police argued that they needed this authorization to prevent serious felonies when they observed a person under circumstances giving them reasonable suspicion the person was about to commit a crime, although no crime had yet been committed.

Chief Justice Earl Warren, who had led the Court to strengthen Fourth Amendment protections, wrote the opinion in *Terry v. Ohio* [1968], which held that it was reasonable under the Fourth Amendment for a police officer to temporarily detain a citizen on the street and inquire into his conduct when the officer had reasonable suspicion that "crime is afoot." Warren rationalized that since these police street stops would occur anyway without much judicial control, it was better for the Court to recognize and regulate them. Justice [John Marshall] Harlan added in his concurring opinion that when an officer reasonably suspected the person was about to commit a felony, the officer should be able not only to seize that person temporarily and make an inquiry but also to immediately pat down the person's clothing to determine if he was armed with a weapon, so that the answer to his inquiry "will not be a bullet."

This well-meaning effort of the Court to dilute Fourth Amendment requirements in the interest of preventing major crime has encouraged law enforcement officers to broaden their intrusion into the ordinary private lives of citizens. Random street stops and frisks, mostly of African American men in urban neighborhoods, have been common under the guise of drug enforcement. Cars are routinely stopped in such areas under the pretext of a broken taillight or the nervous reaction of a nonwhite driver at the sight of a patrol car.

The Supreme Court has upheld this unreasonably intrusive police action on the basis of any slight technically supported excuse of the police, ruling out any consideration of the actual improper motives of the officers involved. The

Court's majority has appeared to be insensitive to the personal humiliation and degradation of the people treated this way by the police. These cases have detoured a great distance from the reasoning of *Terry v. Ohio* and have made the principles of that case practically unrecognizable. They also have persuaded the attorney general that he is justified in authorizing the sweeping up of Muslim immigrants and detaining them in prison.

Dragnet Strategies

The attorney general has also sought to launch two other dragnet strategies to identify potential terrorists. In doing so, he has either forgotten or ignored similar abusive government investigative practices of the past that were exposed by Congress and brought shame and censure on the FBI and other government intelligence agencies.

In a totalitarian state where individual freedom has been snuffed out, the attorney general's plans would have a simple logic.

He has authorized federal agents to infiltrate houses of worship, social meetings, and other gatherings of American citizens to detect any sign of potential terrorist activity. The attorney general claims that if the public can attend such gatherings, an FBI agent also should be able to attend, even in the absence of any proof of wrongdoing. Logical? Yes, but this logic is completely divorced from any basic understanding of the tradition and history of freedom and individual liberty in the United States and of what constitutional restrictions on government action are all about.

The plan also ignores common sense and the pervasive fear that would threaten the free assembly of Americans, whether in houses of worship or social gatherings. We value free expression of ideas in our democracy, which is encouraged and protected by our Constitution. However, in a time of suspicion and fear, the public's knowledge that FBI agents may be present at its meetings would surely chill, if not suffocate, free expression.

The attorney general has offered a parallel plan to identify potential terrorists that is equally insensitive to American values. He wants to create a nationwide network of private informers under a program called TIPS (Terrorism Information and Prevention System). Under this plan, mail carriers, meter readers, and others who have access to private homes would be asked to watch for signs of potential terrorists and report them to federal agents. The attorney general has asked all Americans to watch their neighbors and report suspicious activity. This proposal received such nationwide protest and criticism that the attorney general was forced to partially abandon it. . . .

Reckless Disregard for Privacy

Attorney General Ashcroft has abandoned caution and safeguards and has adopted the rejected and discredited tactics of J. Edgar Hoover's Cointelpro[1] by authorizing federal agents to engage in dragnet infiltration of innocent private organizations and groups without having any reason to believe that there has been or is about to be any violation of federal criminal law.

The attorney general's new domestic intelligence program seeks to reassure us that FBI spies will not misuse information they obtain in this way because he has ordered that such information not be disseminated to law enforcement agents unless it is related to a violation of federal criminal law. However, this is no protection at all. The attorney general misses the point of why the nation rejected Cointelpro. The harm to free expression, free worship, and free dissent has already been done by the federal agent's unsupported presence as a government spy.

Total Information Awareness

More recently, as a new method to determine who among us in America are terrorists, the Pentagon proudly announced a plan called Total Information Awareness to develop a database on the private lives of all Americans. Worse, put in charge of this new operation was former admiral John Poindexter,

---

1. counterintelligence program, a covert FBI operation aimed at the protest movements of the 1960s

notorious for having been convicted by a federal criminal trial jury for lying to Congress about the illegal arms-for-hostages secret plan of the Reagan administration, known as Iran/Contra. As first announced, Poindexter said the plan would cull information from telephone records, credit card purchases, gun purchases, arrests, rental car records, airline reservations, medical files, education reports, and many other files and records covering millions of Americans.

Poindexter resigned his Pentagon position after Congress, which has been complacently giving way to other restrictions on liberty, balked at this one. In an appropriations bill, it scuttled the Pentagon plan and barred further action on it by the executive branch without prior consultation with Congress. The *Hartford Courant* editorialized, "The Orwellian proposal, coined Total Information Awareness, was devised by John Poindexter, the navy rear admiral who helped create a plan in the 1980's to illegally send money to Nicaraguan rebels. . . . Many lawmakers were justifiably outraged at the implications of an extensive data base on every American."

Put together, these sweeping new investigative powers initiated by the federal government are nothing short of frightening and are clearly incompatible with a free society—even in a time of crisis involving the security of the country. Reasonable people can and do differ on how much freedom we as Americans should surrender in time of war or war-like conditions. Most agree that certain restrictions can be tolerated without losing the basic quality of constitutional liberty. However, the determination of its necessity and efficacy must be at the heart of any such restriction.

Law Enforcement Already Has Sufficient Powers

Do federal law enforcement officers really need these expanded powers to engage in effective investigations and prosecutions of terrorists in our midst? There is ample evidence that they do not. Congressional investigations into how our intelligence agencies and the Department of Justice failed to be more prepared for the terrorist attacks on 9/11 point more to incompetence than lack of investigative powers or resources. The strong arsenal of federal law enforcement investigative powers—all granted by Congress and the Supreme Court to law enforcement agencies prior to the attorney general's demand for expanded powers—has been shown to fully allow competent law enforcement officers and prosecutors to successfully protect the country's security against criminal extremists and terrorists.

Professor Philip B. Heymann of Harvard Law School has persuasively demonstrated this capability of law enforcement agencies under the laws and investigative powers existing before 9/11. His book *Terrorism and America* was published in 1998, three years before 9/11, but it is a prophetic manual for meeting the enforcement problems of 9/11 terrorism today. Heymann served as assistant attorney general, chief of the criminal division of the U.S. Department of Justice, during the Jimmy Carter administration and as deputy attorney general, the number-two spot at Justice, during the Clinton administration.

Heymann illustrates his claim that law enforcement officials have sufficient powers under existing law to investigate and prosecute terrorists by describing the successful investigation of the bombing of the World Trade Center in 1993. The investigation, he writes, started at the crime scene, in the crater that the bomb had created, with an army of meticulous searchers. The agents and officers talked to witnesses as quickly as they could be located. Hotlines were immediately established, and rewards were offered. Police were asked to tell the agents of any arrests or traffic stops near the time of the explosion. Agents checked whether there had been any threatening calls or any other messages that might hold clues.

A wider search for evidence involved a review of all recorded information from the pay phones in the area, from all the security video cameras scanning the area at banks and other businesses, and from intelligence and law enforcement agencies that might have picked up something that could be helpful. Heymann describes how the agents checked with informants and carefully reviewed tapes looking for clues of any past electronic surveillance by groups that might have been responsible. Any physical evidence that might have helped was sent immediately to FBI laboratories and was promptly processed. This meticulous collection of evidence led to the discovery of a tiny scrap of the rented vehicle that was enough of a lead to enable the FBI to trace the vehicle to a rental agency, ultimately opening up the leads to identify the bombers. "The case was solved," Heymann writes, "by an intensive use of familiar investigative techniques." He concludes,

> It is obvious from the success of the World Trade Center investigation and of the related investigation of the conspiracy to bomb other sites in the New York area, the conviction of Timothy McVeigh for bombing the federal building in Oklahoma City, and the capture of the "Unabomber," Theodore Kaczynski, that the United States has been able to find evidence and prosecute terrorists' bombings under existing rules for investigation and trial. In each case, massive resources have been directed to the solution of the crimes, but it has not been necessary to change the rules.

This same conclusion can be made concerning the arrests and prosecutions since 9/11 of persons connected in some way to the al Qaeda terrorists. None of the expanded powers of surveillance, searches, or investigations acquired by the attorney general were needed. Yet the existence of these powers and their threatened use by law enforcement officials have created an atmosphere of fear and suspicion throughout the country and have doubtless had a chilling effect on free expression of ideas and dissent among the people.

Freedom Is Our Shield

If the goal of the terrorists is, as President Bush has declared, to destroy the United States as a free and democratic nation, then the federal government's panicked rush to needlessly restrict the liberties of American citizens has provided the terrorists with a victory. A successful war on the terrorists requires quite the opposite strategy. The United States must show the terrorists that the liberty and freedom of its people are its impregnable shield and sword. These essential qualities of a free society have enabled us to flourish economically as a powerful nation and militarily as an invincible champion of democracy.

The wonderful thing about this challenge is that we do not have to create anything—we already have it. Freedom is our heritage from the birth of our nation. It is inscribed in our living Constitution that was so bravely created and has so miraculously endured.

As a people who are the ultimate sovereign in America, we must insist that our government leaders reflect our pride and trust in the American values of liberty and freedom. Our leaders should protect them and rely on them, rather than distrust them as not strong enough to preserve American security. Our government leaders—executive, legislative, and judicial branches—have made many mistakes in the past when they have lost sight of the sacred American values rooted in the Declaration of Independence and the Constitution. We are at the brink of even graver mistakes and assaults on these values. We dare not turn away from them—for how naked, weak, and poor we will be without them.

The Patriot Act Does Not Threaten Fourth Amendment Rights

Viet D. Dinh

In the wake of the September 11, 2001, terrorist attacks, Congress passed the Patriot Act in order to give federal agencies more powers and greater coordination in finding and prosecuting suspected terrorists. Since then, the act has come under virulent criticism from those who believe it is a threat to civil liberties and the protection of privacy. Critics charge that the government will be able to sweep aside citizens' Fourth Amendment protections merely by asserting that they are suspected of terrorism. Opponents also claim that government powers to search through personal information, including library records, will have a chilling effect on freedom of speech and the exchange of ideas. For Viet D. Dinh, a Vietnamese refugee who became a professor of law and a constitutional scholar, these fears are unfounded: Contrary to the assertions of critics, Congress did not rush this legislation through but deliberated on it over six weeks and carefully framed it to protect vital liberties while enhancing equally vital police powers. Indeed, many provisions simply give federal agents powers already used by state and local police forces. Others provide uniform standards and commonsense methods for agencies to pool their knowledge. Far from threatening liberty, according to Dinh, the Patriot Act provides rational, limited tools for fighting terrorism, the greatest threat to liberty Americans face.

Viet D. Dinh, *How the USA Patriot Act Defends Democracy.* Washington, DC: The Foundation for the Defense of Democracies, June 2004. Copyright © 2003 by The Foundation for the Defense of Democracies. Reproduced by permission.

Passed soon after the terrorist attacks of 9/11, the USA Patriot Act is one of the most important legislative measures in American history. The Act enables the government to fight what will undoubtedly be a long and difficult war against international terrorism. At the same time, the Act constrains the government, preventing any government attempt to unjustifiably extend its powers.

Yet the Patriot Act, despite its near-unanimous passage through Congress, has also become one of the most vilified pieces of legislation in living memory. Critics charge that the Act allows for extensive domestic surveillance of US citizens engaged in peaceful, law-abiding activities, that the Act could potentially turn the US into a police state. While some of the rhetoric deployed against the Patriot Act is hyperbolic, the concerns expressed about official surveillance of US citizens are reasonable and should be addressed. The vehemence of many of those who oppose the Patriot Act is a reflection of their attachment to our Constitution, even if, as this paper will argue, many of their fears about government surveillance are unfounded.

Rather than reply to the crescendo of complaints and exaggerated claims in kind, what is needed is a constructive conversation about security and liberty, about the success of our terrorism prevention efforts and the need to protect and defend American freedom. We need to assess the experience of past years to ensure both that officials have the tools necessary to protect us and that there are safeguards to check against misuse of those tools. The national debate will be constructive if we can lower the heat and turn up the light.

Using Security to Protect Liberty

The fundamental question facing Americans today is not the false trade off between security and liberty, but rather how we can use security to protect liberty. Any debate over security and liberty must start with the recognition that the primary threat to American freedom comes from al-Qaeda and other groups that seek to kill Americans, not from the men and women of law enforcement agencies who protect them from that danger. That the American homeland has not suffered another terrorist attack since September 11, 2001, is a testament to the remarkable efforts of law enforcement, intelligence, and homeland security personnel. Their hard work, dedication and increased coordination have been greatly aided by the tools, resources and guidance that Congress provided in the Patriot Act.

To appreciate the difficulty of counterterrorism and the remarkable success of our officials, one need only recount the IRA's [Irish Republican Army's] statement in 1984 after it had tried unsuccessfully to assassinate British prime minister Margaret Thatcher: "Today we were unlucky, but remember we only have to be lucky once. You will have to be lucky always."

Our counterterrorism measures have not been solely defensive. We have taken the offensive. According to the Department of Justice, the US government has disrupted over 100 terrorist cells and incapacitated over 3,000 al-Qaeda operatives worldwide. The Department of Justice has indicted on criminal charges 305 persons linked to terrorism, of whom 176 have entered guilty pleas or been convicted. In addition, the US government has initiated 70 investigations into terrorism financing, freezing $133 million in terrorist assets, and has obtained 23 convictions or guilty pleas.

Counterterrorism has not just been about law enforcement but also law enhancement. Many of the successes of the police and FBI would not have been possible without the Patriot Act. The Department of Justice wrote to the House of Representatives' Judiciary Committee on May 13, 2003, that the government's success in preventing another catastrophic attack on the American homeland "would have been much more difficult, if not impossibly so, without the Patriot Act."

Uncle Sam Is Not Watching You

What is odd about the current debate over the Patriot Act and its surveillance provisions is that this legislation resulted from considerable informed debate. Contrary to popular myth, the Patriot Act was not rushed onto the statute books. During the six weeks of deliberations that led to the passage of the Act, the drafters heard from, and heeded the advice of, a coalition of concerned voices urging caution and care in crafting the blueprint for America's security. That discussion was productive and the Act benefited from these expressions of concern.

More recently, however, the quality of the debate has deteriorated. The shouting voices are ignoring questions that are critical to both security and liberty. Lost among the understandable fears about what the government could be doing are the facts about what the government actually is doing. Overheated rhetoric over minor legal alterations has overshadowed profoundly important questions about fundamental changes in law and policy.

There has been widespread condemnation of Section 215 of the Patriot Act, the so-called "library records" provision. The debate over Section 215 illustrates how awry the direction of the debate has gone. Critics have railed against the provision as allowing a return to J. Edgar Hoover's monitoring of private citizens' reading habits. The American Civil Liberties Union (ACLU) has sued the government, claiming that the provision, through its mere existence, foments a chilling fear among Muslim organizations and activists. Others, more fancifully, have claimed that Section 215 allows the government to act as Big Brother, snooping on innocent citizens in a manner reminiscent of George Orwell's [novel] "1984."

Unfounded Fears

These fears are sincere. They are also historically and legally unfounded. Not only does the Patriot Act end the anomaly that allows such records to be routinely seen by investigators in criminal cases while preventing their access by counter-terrorism officials, the legislation provides more protections than usually occurs when records are subject to subpoena. For years, Grand Juries have issued subpoenas to businesses to hand over records relevant to criminal inquiries. Section 215 of the Patriot Act gives courts, for national security investigations, the same power to issue similar orders to businesses, from chemical makers to explosives dealers. Section 215 is not aimed at bookstores or libraries. Like its criminal grand jury equivalent, Section 215 orders are written with business records in mind but could, if necessary, be applied to reading materials acquired by a terrorist suspect.

Contrary to what the critics claim, Section 215 is narrow in scope. The FBI cannot use Section 215 to investigate garden-variety crimes, nor even domestic terrorism. Instead, Section 215 can be used only to "obtain foreign intelligence information not concerning a United States person," or to "protect against international terrorism or clandestine intelligence activities." The records of average Americans, and even not-so-average criminals, are simply beyond the reach of Section 215.

The fact that Section 215 applies uniquely to national security investigations means that the orders are confidential. As such secrecy raises legitimate concerns, Congress embedded significant checks into the issuing [of] Section 215 warrants. First, a federal judge alone can issue and supervise a Section 215 order. By contrast, Grand Jury subpoenas for records are routinely issued by the court clerk. Second, the government must report to Congress every six months the number of times, and the manner, of the provision's use. On October 17, 2002, the House Judiciary Committee stated that its review of the information "has not given rise to any concern that the authority is being misused or abused." Moreover, in September 2003, the Attorney General made public the previously classified information that Section 215 had not been used once since its passage.

Library and Bookstore Records

It may well be that the clamor over Section 215 reflects a different concern, closely related to the cherished American tradition of free speech. Some seem to fear the government can use ordinary criminal investigative tools to easily obtain records from purveyors of First Amendment activities, such as libraries and bookstores. Again the fundamental concern is as understandable as the specific fear related to Section 215 is unjustified. The prohibition in Section 215 that investigations "not be conducted of a United States person solely upon the basis of activities protected by the first amendment of the Constitution of the United States" addresses this problem directly and makes the Patriot Act more protective of civil liberties than ordinary criminal procedure.

Arguably this limitation should be extended to other investigative tools. The Attorney General's guidelines governing criminal and terrorist investigations already require that "such investigations not be based solely on activities protected by the First Amendment or on the lawful exercise of any other rights secured by the Constitution or laws of the United States." Congress might wish to consider codifying this requirement in law, but that is an entirely different debate to the alleged erosion of liberty by Section 215 and the utility of this restricted power.

Search Warrants

A good example of how the Patriot Act incorporates protections is Section 213, which deals with notices for search warrants. The House of Representatives in July 2003 took the alarming decision to approve the Otter amendment, an appropriations rider that would have prohibited investigators from asking a court to delay notice to a suspect of a search warrant. Had the Otter amendment become law, it would have been a momentous error that would have crippled federal investigations. The amendment would have taken away an investigative tool that had existed before the Patriot Act, a tool that over the years has saved lives and preserved evidence.

Inherent in a federal judge's power to issue a search warrant is the authority to supervise the terms of its use. Judges can delay any notice of the execution of a search warrant for the obvious reason that some criminals, if notified early, will destroy evidence, kill witnesses or simply flee. This judicial authority is firmly established. The Supreme Court in 1979 labeled as "frivolous" an argument that notice of a search warrant had to be immediate. Even the generally permissive Ninth Federal Circuit Court of Appeals has consistently recognized that notice of a warrant may be delayed for a reasonable period of time.

The problem has been that while a judge's right to delay the execution of a warrant is acknowledged, judges have exercised their discretion to delay warrant notice in very different ways. The result is a mix of inconsistent rules and practices across the US. Congress resolved this problem by adopting a uniform standard in Section 213 of the Patriot Act. The section allows a judge to delay notice for a reasonable period only if investigators show "reasonable cause," such as to prevent risk to human life or safety, flight from prosecution, evidence tampering, witness intimidation, or trial delay.

Uniform Standards and Pooled Intelligence

While the Patriot Act finally sets a uniform standard for delaying warrants, thereby evening out the idiosyncratic decisions of the judiciary, it continues to make these delays subject to judicial approval. The uniform "reasonable cause" standard is similar to the Supreme Court's reasonableness test for deciding the circumstances surrounding the service of a warrant. For example, the Supreme Court in December 2003 unanimously approved as reasonable that police enter into a drug house 15 seconds after announcing their presence. Again, the criticism that the Patriot Act extends government powers is inconsistent with the facts of legal practice.

One of the most serious criticisms after 9/11 was that US security agencies failed to pool intelligence that could have prevented the attacks. The Patriot Act addressed this issue while being sensitive to concerns about the capabilities these agencies have for monitoring citizens. Section 218 of the Act amended the Foreign Intelligence Surveillance Act (FISA) to facilitate increased cooperation between agents gathering intelligence about foreign threats and investigators prosecuting foreign terrorists—liaison previously barred by administrative and judicial interpretations of FISA. Even the most strident of opponents of the Patriot Act would not want another terrorist attack to occur because a quarter of a century–old provision prevented the law enforcement and intelligence communities from talking to each other.

Section 218, essential as it is, raises important questions about law enforcement and domestic intelligence. The drafters of the Act grappled with questions such as whether the change is consistent with the Fourth Amendment protection against unreasonable search and seizure, whether criminal prosecutors should initiate and direct intelligence operations and whether there is adequate process for defendants to seek exclusion of intelligence evidence from their trial. In the end, Congress decided that Section 218 complies with the Fourth Amendment and that defendants have sufficient recourse to exclude evidence gathered by intelligence agencies from their trials. Although the drafters felt that they had struck the correct balance, they recognized that lawyers are fallible and that the courts will ultimately decide. In November 2002, the Foreign Intelligence Surveillance Court of Review decided that the provision was fully consistent with the Constitution.

A Shield of American Democracy

The Patriot Act's surveillance provisions are not the executive grab for power and extension of government that many portray them to be. Rather the Act sensibly updates the law to keep pace with changing technology, tidies up confused legal interpretations and standardizes powers while restraining them. The Act gives the government the tools it needs to fight terrorism while observing the cherished liberties of Americans. Counterterrorism is a dynamic process, and the Patriot Act is not written in stone. It will be scrutinized by the courts, debated by the citizenry and amended by Congress.

We have to recognize that our nation is navigating uncharted waters. We have been forced to fight an unprovoked conflict, a war declared against us by nihilistic terrorists, not by our traditional adversary, a nation-state. During these times, when the foundation of liberty is under attack, it is critical that we both reaffirm the ideals of our constitutional democracy and also discern the techniques necessary to secure those ideals against the threat of terrorism. As Karl Llewellyn, the renowned law professor, once observed: "Ideals without technique are a mess. But technique without ideals is a menace." The Patriot Act, by combining ideals and technique, is the domestic shield of American democracy, a protection deserving of renewal by our Congress.

The Origins of the American Bill of Rights

The U.S. Constitution as it was originally created and sub-mitted to the colonies for ratification in 1787 did not include what we now call the Bill of Rights. This omission was the cause of much controversy as Americans debated whether to accept the new Constitution and the new federal government it created. One of the main concerns voiced by opponents of the document was that it lacked a detailed listing of guaran-tees of certain fundamental individual rights. These critics did not succeed in preventing the Constitution's ratification, but were in large part responsible for the existence of the Bill of Rights.

In 1787 the United States consisted of thirteen former British colonies that had been loosely bound since 1781 by the Articles of Confederation. Since declaring their inde-pendence from Great Britain in 1776, the former colonies had established their own colonial governments and consti-tutions, eight of which had bills of rights written into them. One of the most influential was Virginia's Declaration of Rights. Drafted largely by planter and legislator George Mason in 1776, the seventeen-point document combined philosophical declarations of natural rights with specific lim-itations on the powers of government. It served as a model for other state constitutions.

The sources for these declarations of rights included En-glish law traditions dating back to the 1215 Magna Carta and the 1689 English Bill of Rights—two historic documents that provided specific legal guarantees of the "true, ancient, and indubitable rights and liberties of the people" of Eng-land. Other legal sources included the colonies' original char-ters, which declared that colonists should have the same "privileges, franchises, and immunities" that they would if they lived in England. The ideas concerning natural rights developed by John Locke and other English philosophers were also influential. Some of these concepts of rights had been cited in the Declaration of Independence to justify the American Revolution.

Unlike the state constitutions, the Articles of Confederation, which served as the national constitution from 1781 to 1788, lacked a bill of rights. Because the national government under the Articles of Confederation had little authority by design, most people believed it posed little threat to civil liberties, rendering a bill of rights unnecessary. However, many influential leaders criticized the very weakness of the national government for creating its own problems; it did not create an effective system for conducting a coherent foreign policy, settling disputes between states, printing money, and coping with internal unrest.

It was against this backdrop that American political leaders convened in Philadelphia in May 1787 with the stated intent to amend the Articles of Confederation. Four months later the Philadelphia Convention, going beyond its original mandate, created a whole new Constitution with a stronger national government. But while the new Constitution included a few provisions protecting certain civil liberties, it did not include any language similar to Virginia's Declaration of Rights. Mason, one of the delegates in Philadelphia, refused to sign the document. He listed his objections in an essay that began:

> There is no Declaration of Rights, and the Laws of the general government being paramount to the laws and constitution of the several States, the Declaration of Rights in the separate States are no security.

Mason's essay was one of hundreds of pamphlets and other writings produced as the colonists debated whether to ratify the new Constitution (nine of the thirteen colonies had to officially ratify the Constitution for it to go into effect). The supporters of the newly drafted Constitution became known as Federalists, while the loosely organized group of opponents were called Antifederalists. Antifederalists opposed the new Constitution for several reasons. They believed the presidency would create a monarchy, Congress would not be truly representative of the people, and state governments would be endangered. However, the argument that proved most effective was that the new document lacked a bill of rights and thereby threatened Americans with the loss of cherished individual liberties. Federalists realized that to gain the support of key states such as New York and Virginia, they needed to pledge to offer amendments to the Constitution that would be added immediately after its ratification. Indeed, it was not until this promise was made that the requisite number of colonies ratified the document. Massachusetts, Virginia, South Carolina, New Hampshire, and New York all included amendment recommendations as part of their decisions to ratify.

One of the leading Federalists, James Madison of Virginia, who was elected to the first Congress to convene under the new Constitution, took the lead in drafting the promised amendments. Under the process provided for in the Constitution, amendments needed to be passed by both the Senate and House of Representatives and then ratified by three-fourths of the states. Madison sifted through the suggestions provided by the states and drew upon the Virginia Declaration of Rights and other state documents in composing twelve amendments, which he introduced to Congress in September 1789. "If they are incorporated into the constitution," he argued in a speech introducing his proposed amendments,

> Independent tribunals of justice will consider themselves in a peculiar manner the guardians of those rights; they will be an impenetrable bulwark against every assumption of power in the legislative or executive; they will be naturally led to resist every encroachment upon rights expressly stipulated for in the constitution by the declaration of rights.

After debate and some changes to Madison's original proposals, Congress approved the twelve amendments and sent them to the states for ratification. Two amendments were not ratified; the remaining ten became known as the Bill of Rights. Their ratification by the states was completed on December 15, 1791.

Supreme Court Cases Involving
Freedom from Unfair Searches and Seizures

1886

Boyd v. United States
The Court ruled that prosecutors cannot compel suspects to hand over self-incriminating documents nor use such documents in court against the defendant's objection.

1914

Weeks v. United States
The Court concluded that evidence obtained illegally by federal officials should be excluded from trial, establishing the so-called exclusionary rule.

1920

Silverthorne Lumber Co. v. United States
The Court ruled that knowledge gained from illegally seized evidence cannot be used to justify a valid subpoena for that same evidence. This ruling ultimately gave rise to the "Fruit of the Poisonous Tree" doctrine, which excludes the use of evidence that itself is only discovered because of other evidence that was obtained illegally.

1921

Gouled v. United States
The Court found that although government may seize illegal materials and materials that are in a suspect's possession only because of a crime (such as stolen goods) the government may not seize "mere evidence" and use it in court. There have been numerous exceptions to this "mere evidence" rule, and as the Court's interest has shifted from property rights to privacy rights much of this ruling's reasoning has been effectively overturned, especially since *Warden v. Hayden*, decided in 1967.

1925

Carroll v. United States
The Court found that it is reasonable for police officers to conduct a warrantless search of a car they have pulled over if they have probable cause for suspecting a crime, establishing the so-called "automobile exception" to the right not to be searched.

1928

Olmstead v. United States
In its first case on wiretaps, the Court ruled that since no physical trespass of a private location was needed to tap a public phone, no warrant was necessary. This ruling was in keeping with the traditional view of the Fourth Amendment, but it was effectively overturned by *Katz v. United States* in 1967.

1947

Harris v. United States
The Court ruled that if legitimately on the premises of a detained suspect, investigators may search the area under the detainee's control but may not conduct "exploratory searches."

1961

Mapp v. Ohio
This ruling extended the exclusionary rule, which bars the use of illegally obtained evidence in trials, to state courts, where the large majority of crimes are tried.

1967

Katz v. United States
This case overturned *Olmstead v. United States*. The Court found that a warrantless search can be unconstitutional even without a physical trespass if it violates a suspect's reasonable expectation of privacy.

Warden v. Hayden

The Court largely overturned the "mere evidence" rule established in *Gouled v. United States* in 1921, which had forbidden officials to seize items that were not specifically tied to the commission of a crime but had a reasonable relation to proving a case. Such "mere evidence" as fingerprints, blood samples, and clothes that identify a suspect can be forcibly seized and used in court under this new ruling.

1968

Terry v. Ohio

The Court concluded that police must obtain warrants in advance whenever practicable, but limited searches for weapons on a detainee—stop and frisk tactics—are reasonable.

1971

Bivens v. Six Unknown Named Agents of
Federal Bureau of Narcotics

The Court ruled that civil damages against officials who violate the Fourth Amendment rights of suspects are still appropriate remedies.

1972

United States v. United States District Court
for Eastern District of Michigan

The Court found that it is not reasonable for the president or the attorney general to use national security concerns to authorize warrantless searches (electronic surveillance).

1974

United States v. Calandra

The Court ruled that the exclusionary rule does not apply to questions and testimony before grand juries.

1976

Stone v. Powell
The Court concluded that if Fourth Amendment issues have been adequately aired and decided in state courts, they do not have to be relitigated in federal courts. The Court went further, ruling that lower courts have some discretion to effectively set aside the exclusionary rule if the costs of excluding evidence would significantly outweigh the benefits. Generally, this ruling has applied to state prisoners asking federal courts to grant them a new trial because of Fourth Amendment violations.

United States v. Janis
The Court found that evidence seized in good faith can be used in a civil proceeding, even if it was originally taken improperly under a defective warrant.

1978

Rakas v. Illinois
The Court ruled that automobile passengers who own neither the car nor its contents do not have a legitimate expectation of privacy and therefore cannot claim a Fourth Amendment violation if items seized by police officers are used against them.

1984

Nix v. Williams
The Court ruled that improperly obtained evidence that would normally be inadmissible under the exclusionary rule can actually be admitted if discovery of the evidence was inevitable without the use of tainted evidence or an improper confession.

United States v. Leon
The Court concluded that a good faith attempt to comply with the Fourth Amendment may be sufficient. If police officers believe they are acting within a legitimate warrant, evidence may be admitted even if the warrant turns out to be improper.

1985

New Jersey v. T.L.O.
The Court found that the Fourth Amendment applies to schools and school officials, although in a more limited way than it applies to police and the general public.

1986

California v. Ciraolo
The Court ruled that aerial surveillance of a backyard by police without a warrant does not violate the Fourth Amendment.

1988

California v. Greenwood
The Court declared that there is no reasonable expectation of privacy for garbage left on the curb for pickup.

1990

United States v. Verdugo-Urquidez
The Court ruled that the Fourth Amendment does not apply to persons and property of nonresident aliens.

1995

Vernonia School District v. Acton
School officials have a right to conduct random urinalysis drug searches of school athletes if they have reasonable suspicion of rampant drug use.

1996

Whren v. United States
The Court found that as long as there is a reasonable basis for a traffic stop, even if it is not the primary reason for the police to stop a car, a subsequent search of the car is permitted. (Narcotics officers had used the pretext of speeding and turning without signaling to stop a driver they suspected of carrying drugs, and prosecutors were allowed to use the seized drugs as evidence against the suspects.)

2001

Kyllo v. United States
The Court concluded that use of a thermal-imaging device to detect heat emissions in a private home, without a warrant, violates suspects' privacy rights.

2002

Board of Education v. Earls
The Court extended its ruling in *Vernonia School District v. Acton*, finding that school districts could mandate drug testing for all students engaged in extracurricular activities.

Books

Ellen Alderman and Caroline Kennedy, *The Right to Privacy.* New York: Vintage, 1997.

Akhil Reed Amar, *The Bill of Rights: Creation and Reconstruction.* New Haven, CT: Yale University Press, 1998.

William Blackstone, *Commentaries on the Laws of England.* Chicago: University of Chicago Press, 1979.

David Brin, *The Transparent Society: Will Technology Force Us to Choose Between Privacy and Freedom?* Reading, PA: Perseus, 1998.

Samuel Dash, *The Eavesdroppers.* New Brunswick, NJ: Rutgers University Press, 1959.

————, *The Intruders: Unreasonable Searches and Seizures from King John to John Ashcroft.* New Bruswick, NJ: Rutgers University Press, 2004.

Viet D. Dinh, *How the USA Patriot Act Defends Democracy.* Washington, DC: The Foundation for the Defense of Democracies, 2004.

The Exclusionary Rule Debate. Chicago: American Judicature Society, 1979.

Ron Felber, *The Privacy War: One Congressman, J. Edgar Hoover, and the Fight for the Fourth Amendment.* Montvale, NJ: Croce, 2003.

Paula Angle Franklin, *The Fourth Amendment.* Englewood Cliffs, NJ: Silver Burdett, 1991.

Brian Glick, *War at Home: Covert Action Against U.S. Activists and What We Can Do About It.* Boston: South End, 1989.

William W. Greenhalgh, *The Fourth Amendment Handbook: A Chronological Survey of Supreme Court Decisions.* Chicago: American Bar Association, 2003.

J. David Hirschel, *Fourth Amendment Rights*. Lexington, MA: Lexington Books, 1979.

Wayne R. LaFave, *Search and Seizure: A Treatise on the Fourth Amendment*. St. Paul, MN: West, 1978.

Jacob W. Landynski, *Search and Seizure and the Supreme Court: A Study in Constitutional Interpretation*. Baltimore: Johns Hopkins Press, 1966.

Nelson B. Lasson, *The History and Development of the Fourth Amendment in the United States Constitution*. Baltimore: Johns Hopkins Press, 1937.

Darien A. McWhirter, *Search, Seizure and Privacy*. Phoenix: Oryx, 1994.

Steven L. Nock, *The Costs of Privacy: Surveillance and Reputation in America*. New York: Aldine de Gruyter, 1993.

Jeffrey Rosen, *The Naked Crowd: Reclaiming Security and Freedom in an Anxious Age*. New York: Random House, 2004.

James B. Rule, *Private Lives and Public Surveillance: Social Control in the Computer Age*. New York: Schocken, 1974.

Steven R. Schlesinger, *Exclusionary Injustice: The Problem of Illegally Obtained Evidence*. New York: Marcel Dekker, 1977.

M.H. Smith, *The Writs of Assistance Case*. Berkeley: University of California Press, 1978.

Robert Ellis Smith, *Ben Franklin's Web Site: Privacy and Curiosity from Plymouth Rock to the Internet*. Providence, RI: Privacy Journal, 2000.

Malcolm Richard Wilkey, *Enforcing the Fourth Amendment by Alternatives to the Exclusionary Rule*. Washington, DC: National Legal Center for the Public Interest, 1982.

Bradford P. Wilson, *Enforcing the Fourth Amendment: A Jurisprudential History*. New York: Garland, 1986.

Priscilla H. Machado Zotti, *Injustice for All: Mapp v. Ohio and the Fourth Amendment*. New York: Peter Lang, 2005.

Web Sites

American Civil Liberties Union, Criminal Justice: Search and Seizure, www.aclu.org. This site provides a regularly updated list of important ACLU lawsuits involving search-and-seizure law as well as press releases and information on threats to Fourth Amendment protections.

FindLaw Constitution Center, www.findlaw.com. A clearinghouse for lawyers, law students, and the public, this site provides links to case law and judicial interpretation of the Constitution and its amendments, including the Fourth Amendment restricting search and seizure.

Flex Your Rights, www.flexyourrights.org. Designed to make citizens aware of their rights against warrantless searches and self-incrimination, this site also provides a brief history of the Fourth Amendment and a page of frequently asked questions concerning police searches.

'Lectric Law Library Web Site, Fourth Amendment, www.lectlaw.com. Designed as an introduction to various legal terms and concepts, the 'Lectric Law Library Web site provides a summary of numerous Fourth Amendment issues—including the legality of fingerprinting, drawing blood from detainees, and searching cars at sobriety checkpoints—that touch on larger search-and-seizure issues.

INDEX